Praise for Diane DiResta and *Knockout Presentations:*

Diane Diresta has managed to reach into her rich background and forge a "how to" life guide which is magical for any person who wants a presentation to become a source of confident pride. Readers will find themselves marking heaps of pages and returning often to freshly absorb Diane's practical, purposeful, pleasing guides to exellence.

—Bob Danzig
Former CEO/Hearst Newspapers
author, professional speaker, professor

This book provides you with a practical approach to handling the most difficult moments in your life—your presentations.... Knockout Presentations goes beyond your presenation skills—it really provides you with the substance to enhance your career.

—Stephen R. Guglielmo
Managing Vice President, Reliance National

Diane DiResta is a knockout on the platform and *Knockout Presentations* surely lives up to her reputation. Fille with PRACTICAL advice and exercises, this book focuses on the "how" and "why" of speaking. I highly recommend it.

—Esther Eagles
Eagles Talent Connection

DiResta is a master at transforming the famous and the not-so-famous into effective, engaging, and credible public speakers. Her communication style and wisdom are lifesavers in a media frenzy or before groups of any size. A must read for every communicator.

—Lee Antonio
Public Relations Manager, Sears, Roebuck, and Co.

Diane DiResta is a consummate professional who has generously shared her expertise with us in this easy-to-read, very informative book.... I whis this book had been available when I started my speaking career.

—Hilka Klinkenberg
Author of *At Ease... Professionally*

DiResta's book is delightful! Whether you're a seasoned speaking professional or just want to deliver a talk to your peers, this is the one book you won't want to be without.

—Jim Donovan
Author of *Handbook to a Happier Life*

From the outset, DiResta places the reader at ease. She knows her audience and her proven techniques are certain to fulfill expectations.

—Gregory J. Sacco
Director of National Accounts, Copesan Services

As one who regularly attends Corporate and Shareholder meetings, I've discovered a cure for insomnia... boring presentations! *Knockout Presentations* should be required reading for every executive.

–Robert Chesney
Executive Producer, *Window on Wall Street*

Knockout Presentations is truly a "how-to" book and will help readers make lasting impressions when presenting.

–Donald Heath,
Director, Training & Career Development
Helena Chemical Company

If you're a subject matter expert, an employee making a first presentation to your team, or a local speaker about to present to a national audience, you'll find dozens of valuable tips in *Knockout Presentations*. You'll need two copies-one to keep for yourself and one to share with colleagues.

–Barbara Sacker
President, Pro-Action, Inc.

*Knockout Presentation*s is a simple, user-friendly, practical guide for anyone who has ever or will ever speak in public.... It's a book that I'll use in planning my own presentations and give out to participants in training sessions on presentation skills.

–Audrey Goodman
Director, Organizational Development
Merck-Medco Managed Care, L.L.C.

This book is like having my own personal coach. Every business executive would benefit from *Knockout Presentations*.

–Steve Carbone
President, Grey Direct E. Marketing

Knockout Presentations gives the reader a practical guide to developing and presenting a message with impact. DiResta encourages you to explore your own style and ways to improve your effectiveness. This book is an important tool to enhance your leadership presence.

–Kathleen Finigan
Principal, The Leadership Board

The techniques learned in *Knockout Presentations* and the confidence gained will be used in every area of life. For me, the single most valuable take away was the ability to structure thoughts into a clear succinct message and then to present them in a manner that is appropriate for both the situation and my personal style.

–Clement Napolitano
Director of Communications
Wagner Scott Mercator, L.L.C.

Knockout Presentations

How to Deliver Your Message with Power, Punch, and Pizzazz

Knockout
Presentations
How to Deliver Your Message with Power, Punch, and Pizzazz

Diane DiResta

Chandler House Press
Worcester, Massachusetts

ISBN 1-886284-25-3
Library of Congress Catalog Card Number 97-72604
First Edition
  CDEFGHIJK

Published by
Chandler House Press
335 Chandler Street
Worcester, MA 01602 USA

President
Lawrence J. Abramoff

Publishing Director
Claire Cousineau

Book Design and Production
CWL Publishing Enterprises
www.cwlpub.com

Cover Design
Marshall Henrichs

Chandler House Press specializes in custom publishing for businesses, organizations, and individuals. For more information on how to publish through our corporation, please contact Chandler House Press, 335 Chandler Street, Worcester, MA 01602. Call (800) 642-6657, fax (508) 756-9425, or find us on the World Wide Web at www.chandlerhousepress.com.

Dedication

To all the students and participants in my seminars, who taught me as much as I taught them. And to my late chihuahua, Yoda, who often sat in my lap as I was writing this book.

Contents

Foreword

*L*ike Diane DiResta's presentation skills programs, this book is
practical, to the point, and powerful. Whether you are a seasoned speaker, heading up the ladder, new in a job, or just wise
enough to know that strong oral communication skills get you
where you want to go in your career and in your life, you will
find this book immediately usable and valuable.

After successfully training thousands of career-minded people
for over 15 years, and watching the need for speaking skills continue to rise, Diane realized there was no really simple and user-
friendly "how-to" book on the subject. Determined to change that
and to prove these skills can be learned (that they are not
"inborn"), she has taken her no-fail techniques and confidence-
building advice and put it to pen for millions more to use.
So if you're pressed for time but want to get ahead, read on and
try out the countless ways to leave your listeners impressed and
nodding, "Yes!"

–Tessa Albert Warschaw, Ph.D.
Author of *Winning by Negotiation*
and *Rich Is Better*

Preface

A national survey was conducted to determine the most commonly held fears people have. Some of the fears respondents identified were of crowded spaces, heights, insects, and elevators. But of all the fears listed in 17 categories, guess which one was cited most often?

Fear of public speaking! It even beat out the fear of death! Some people would rather die than give a speech!
I have personally surveyed hundreds of participants in my seminars to find out why they are afraid to speak in public. The most frequently given reasons are as follows:

- Afraid of appearing foolish.
- Fear of losing train of thought.
- Don't like being the center of attention.
- Don't like their appearance.
- "I'm not a good speaker."
- "I don't know what to say."
- "My voice shakes."
- "I turn red."

It seems that people are afraid of humiliation. Furthermore, they think that public speaking ability is some magical genetic trait that only a select few are lucky to receive from their parents.

The myth is that good speakers are born. The truth is that good speakers are made. Gifted speakers are born. Martin Luther

King, Ronald Reagan, Jesse Jackson, and Maya Angelou were blessed with a God-given talent that they maximized through much training and practice.Not everyone is gifted. But anyone—including you—can be an effective public speaker.

The Story of Bill

Bill was referred to me by one of my clients. He was a young entrepreneur and had to deliver a speech in two days. His partner didn't think Bill should be speaking because he didn't do a good job at a prior presentation. My assignment was to coach Bill on his laptop computer presentation.

We worked for two hours on his delivery skills and tweaked his organization. Bill then rushed off to catch a plane and made some last-minute changes on the flight. When he arrived at his hotel, he practiced his presentation using the coaching techniques we'd worked on together.

A couple of weeks later, I received an excited call from Bill. He told me how well his second presentation had gone, and he faxed me the results. Bill's customer confided that he had delayed giving Bill feedback from the first presentation because it had not been very good. Here's the feedback Bill received before and after coaching:

Before coaching	After coaching
Overall score of 2.6 (on a 1-5 scale)	Overall score of 4.0 (on a 1-5 scale)
Written comments:	*Written comments:*
Poor presentation skills	Speaker was very clear
Delivery hard to follow	Entertaining, informative
Confusing	Great info, a bit too fast
Disorganized	Excellent, effective visual aids
Knows subject, poor speaker	Broad, deep knowledge

As Bill found out, effective presenting is simply a matter of learning and mastering the proper skills. First you have to conquer your fears. Then you can learn the skills, apply them, and benefit from them. When you learn a skill, you develop awareness. As you practice that skill, you develop mastery. With mastery comes confidence. With confidence comes a sense of control. And having a sense of mastery and control helps you conquer the fear.

I was terrified when I skied for the first time. I was afraid I would crash and hurt myself because I didn't know how to stop. As soon as I picked up speed, I would cause myself to fall. After going downhill head first, several times, I realized there had to be a better way. Then I learned to snowplow. This skill gave me a sense of control. I'm not a great skier but I can now get down the hill without falling.

It's the same with public speaking. By learning the appropriate steps and skills, and practicing them, you will have a sense of control. If you get into trouble, you'll know how to recover. Most important, you will no longer avoid one of the most important skills for career success. The ability to communicate and be visible in an organization is necessary for job promotion and career mobility. According to Harvey MacKay, author of book *Swim with the Sharks*, "The No. 1 skill most lacking in business today is public speaking—the ability to present oneself."

I once spoke at a women's conference on the topic of Present with Power. I felt it went well. Afterward, I listened to the comments of the crowd. One woman was discussing my presentation. She said, "I thought she was good, but I don't public speak." This woman missed the point. She does speak in public!

Everyone is a public speaker. Any time you speak up at a meeting, talk to a circle of friends, or train your colleagues to perform a task, you're speaking in public.

What's the difference between situations like these and situations you might think of as "formal" public speaking engagements? Well, in your "everyday" public speaking situations, you feel comfortable with the people and you know your subject.

So how do you create that same comfort zone when you're giving a "formal" speech or presentation? I recommend the **YAM** formula:

- Know **Yourself**,
- Know your **Audience**, and
- Know your **Material**.

It's that simple! Everything we're going to talk about in this book falls into one of these categories.

But you cannot improve your public speaking and presentation skills by simply being a passive reader of this book. On the contrary, this book will challenge you to take an active role as we work together. This book is interactive. There are exercises, checklists, and surveys for you to complete.

This book is your experimental lab. You cannot make a mistake. You're simply trying on new behaviors. Some will suit you. Others won't fit. Take what works and start applying it immediately.

Let's begin. Together, we're going to take the mystery out of public speaking and give you the skills and confidence you need to present with power, punch, and pizzazz.

Special Features

There are some special features I've included to make this book more useful to you.

- **Exercises.** Spread throughout the book are a variety of exercises. They're in shaded boxes and ask you to do some activity that will help you master the ideas in that part of the book. Try them. They'll help you achieve the proficiency you're seeking.
- **Case Studies.** Also found in shaded boxes, these provide anecdotes to help enliven and exemplify principles and techniques.

Acknowledgments

Thank you to Dick Staron and Irene Bergman of Chandler House Press for publishing my first book.

Pegine Echevarria, author of *For All Our Daughters*, put me in touch with Chandler House Press so that *Knockout Presentations* could become a reality.

A special thank you to Don Gabor, author of several books, including *How to Start a Conversation and Make Friends*, for mentoring me through the writing process. He gave unselfishly of his time and encouraged me to honor each small achievement. As a veteran author, his advice was practical, timely, and accurate.

At CWL Publishing Enterprises, Peter Vogt and Robert Magnan edited the manuscript, Dale Mann created the chapter-opening cartoons, and John Woods designed and produced the book you now hold. I want to thank them for their help.

The National Speakers Association continues to provide an unlimited supply of resources and a community of positive thinkers. It is one of my greatest support systems.

Most importantly, a special thank-you goes to Janet FitzGerald, my close friend and associate, who encouraged me and convinced me I could write. An excellent writer herself, she took time to critique my writing and always had time for an encouraging word. Everyone needs someone to believe in them and Janet is a true believer.

Finally, thanks to you for buying this book. Read it, learn from it, and have fun with it. And then go out and deliver a knockout presentation!

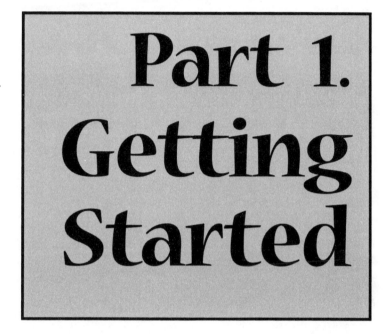

Part 1.
Getting
Started

Secrets of Platform Effectiveness

*A journey of a thousand miles begins
with a single step.*
−Confucius

*T*here are many misconceptions about how to speak effectively to an audience. People look for formulas and rules to follow with the belief that public speaking is a mechanical process. It's not; it's a human process. Other people think they could never become a public speaker—they just have no talent. While exceptional speakers usually do have a real talent for it, this doesn't mean that we all can't give a speech that will engage our audience and be a personally rewarding experience at the same time. The book you hold in your hands is all about helping you do that. But before we get into all the how-to's, let's review some of the major myths about public speaking and dispel them.

Public Speaking: Dispelling the Top Ten Myths

The more you hold onto old—and often misguided—beliefs about public speaking, the less effective you'll be on the platform. You must go in with an open mind and, in some cases, work to change your thinking about giving presentations.

As we start this process of helping you become a better presenter and speaker, it's important that you start with a clean slate. With that in mind, here are ten of the most common myths about public speaking—along with some food for thought to help you dispel the myths in your own mind.

1. I'm not a public speaker. Wrong. Everyone is a public speaker. Every time you speak at a staff meeting, you're speaking in public. Anytime you stand up and introduce yourself at an association meeting, you're giving a presentation. The waiter who recites the specials of the day is presenting. When you complain to the customer service department or go on a job interview, you're presenting yourself.
Reality: We all speak in public. Public speaking goes far beyond standing on a stage in front of 100 people. We're presenting ourselves all the time. In fact, life is one big presentation.

2. Don't speak with your hands. This myth surfaces in many of my presentation skills seminars. One person confided that her father had told her never to talk with her hands. His experience was that people would think she was an immigrant. Think about yourself in a one-to-one conversation. We all talk with our hands. We're just not conscious of it.

Reality: Expressive, dynamic speakers use their hands. Speakers who don't use any hand movement appear stiff. So let your hands speak for themselves!

3. Look over the heads of the audience. Another variation on this myth is to stare at a spot on the wall instead of looking at your audience. You may have heard that these strategies will reduce your nervousness when presenting. But either technique will only increase your nervousness. You'll quickly begin to feel alienated from your audience. Would you meet a person face to face and stare over that person's head?

Reality: Look directly at key individuals. We connect with each other through our eyes. Effective speakers look at a few people, one at a time. This creates a relationship, and it's less scary giving your message to each person than to a large crowd.

4. Memorize your speech. Memorizing your presentation word for word increases your nervousness. What happens if you blank out and forget a word? You'll have to quickly skim your text or tolerate long, embarrassing silences.

Reality: It's more effective to memorize concepts, not words. If you forget a word, you can make your point another way or go on to a new point. Your audience will not know the difference. When possible, avoid using manuscripts. Notes and outlines will better help you to stay on track.

5. Stand in one place. While you don't want to pace all over the platform, you don't have to make yourself a human totem pole. Some speakers think that they have to retreat behind a lectern, like a turtle hides inside its shell.

Reality: Purposeful movement can be dynamic. Watch some of the top motivational speakers, like Zig Ziglar, Tony Robbins, and Les Brown. They work the crowd. They move across the platform. By doing this, you'll increase the energy in the audience.

6. Always use a lectern. Most people love the lectern because they can use it as a crutch and hide behind it.

Reality: There's only one reason to use a lectern: to hold your notes. Use a lectern only when you have to speak from a manuscript. Otherwise, you risk giving a presentation that will be perceived as formal and stiff.

7. Cover all your points in your speech. Most speakers buy into this myth. They have so much to give the audience that they cram all the information into the allotted time. The result: information overload for the audience members.

Reality: Consider the time frame and modify your talk. Give three major points instead of six. Condense your examples. Tell shorter stories. People will be more likely to remember your speech if you take this approach instead of trying to squeeze too much into too short a window of time.

8. Start with a joke. While humor is important, it's different from comedy. If you're not a "natural" at telling jokes, you might alienate the audience. Even if you're good at telling jokes, you almost always risk offending or perhaps confusing someone.

Reality: Don't do it. You don't have to be funny to be effective. Use humor or irony instead of telling a joke. Or, simply start with a story or a quote. Throw away the jokes. More often than not, they backfire.

9. Shut the lights off to show slides. Many presenters blacken the room when presenting with overheads or slides. They believe this will increase visual clarity and command attention.

Reality: In total darkness, your audience members will fall asleep. And they'll be startled when you turn the lights back on. Use a dimmer instead. Give people enough light to see the slides, and be sure you can see their faces as well.

10. You shouldn't be nervous. Says who? Most people come to presentation skills seminars because they want to eliminate nervousness.

Reality: You can control and manage your nervousness, but you can't eliminate it. For most of us, the fear of making presentations never really goes away. Even the top speakers get nervous. But some nervous energy is good for you. It keeps you dynamic. The goal is to channel your nervous energy into a positive performance. (See Chapter 3 for strategies to help you control nervousness during your presentations.)

Exercise

> Maybe you have some preconceived notions about how to speak publicly. Write down those beliefs here. Where did these beliefs come from? (Example: Don't talk with your hands. My boss told me it wasn't professional.) Based on what you just read, are they helping or hindering you? My beliefs:
>
> _____
>
> _____
>
> _____
>
> _____

The Most Common Mistakes Speakers Make

Whenever you're presenting, you're going to make mistakes. Sometimes the mistakes you make on the public speaking platform result from your belief in one or more of the myths described above. At other times, your mistakes might stem from your ignorance or inexperience.

Whatever the case, here are some of the most common mistakes speakers make. We'll examine the solutions in later sections of the book.

1. Lack of preparation. If you're unprepared as a speaker, it shows. You must take the time to know your topic and to rehearse your presentation until you're comfortable with it. If you're unprepared, you'll look unprofessional. Practice your speech out loud and be prepared for questions afterward.

2. Lateness. Starting and ending your presentation late shows a lack of respect for the audience. People have busy schedules. If your presentation is going to be delayed, make sure it's not because of you. Allow time to get to your presentation early, and know how to cut and summarize the presentation if you sense you're running out of time.

3. Not knowing the audience. One of the biggest mistakes you can make as a presenter is not meeting the needs of your audience. It's a great way to turn an otherwise receptive group into a hostile one. Don't talk over people's heads, but don't be too simplistic either. If you're giving the same speech to different groups, tailor it for each audience.

4. Projecting the wrong image. This is an instant credibility killer, and it's related to mistake No. 3. A flashy outfit will not work if you're speaking to bankers. A slick, "big city" style doesn't do it for farmers in Kansas. Study the audience ahead of time and dress and present appropriately.

5. Using visual aids ineffectively. If you fumble with visual aids, you'll eventually lose your credibility. Visuals should support and enhance the presentation, not take it over. Similarly, equipment that malfunctions can be disastrous to the speech. Check out all of your equipment before you speak, and have a backup plan in case the equipment fails.

6. Including too much material. More is better, right? Not really. You can overwhelm the audience with too much data. Don't give them soup to nuts if you don't have enough time. People can't digest information if you give them too much to chew on, so give them the condensed version. If you do, you'll make your points more easily and be more memorable.

7. Using inappropriate humor. This mistake is also related to mistake No. 3. The mores concerning humor have changed. Audiences are politically sensitive. All it takes is one questionable joke or statement to turn people off. Never tell off-color jokes. The best bet is to poke fun at yourself—or avoid jokes altogether

8. Being a monotone. Audience members will be bored if you're a monotone speaker. Too many speakers fail to realize the importance the tone of their voice plays in the success of their presentation.

9. Not building a relationship with the audience. To be effective as a speaker, you must connect with your audience. If you're self-absorbed and you simply recite a speech, you'll soon be talking in a vacuum. No one will be listening.

10. Lacking in focus. Often presenters have an interesting topic that's difficult to follow. That's because they themselves aren't sure where they're going with the presentation. Be clear in your purpose and focus, and make sure that your major points support that purpose.

11. Starting with details. Be careful not to get into details too early in your presentation. Doing so only causes confusion. People need a clear beginning, middle, and end. Give them the big picture or overview in the introduction and save the details for the body of the speech.

12. Being speaker-centered. Too many presenters start with their own agenda and then wonder why they don't get the desired response from the audience. Surprisingly, many salespeople are speaker-centered. They're so interested in pushing their product that they forget about the buyer's needs. Begin your presentation from the listener's point of view and continue to address what's important to them.

13. Offering only weak evidence. Some speakers don't support their ideas with solid data or evidence. They expect the audience to take things on faith. If your presentation is sketchy or lacks substance, flesh it out and fill in the details. It's not enough to present your points; you must build a case. How? By including statistics, personal stories, examples, analogies, demonstrations, pictures, testimonials, conceptual models, and historical data. Construct a frame, then build the house.

Present or Perish! Why You Must Have Presentation Skills

You can no longer avoid developing your skill in making effective presentations. Public speaking is one of the most powerful marketing tools today. Companies and organizations realize that in an increasingly competitive market, it is their presentation that makes them stand out from the crowd. And as technology grows, the ability to convey data in a clear, simple manner is becoming an even more valuable skill.

Ours is a verbal, extroverted society, generally speaking. The ability to express ourselves through language is what makes us uniquely human. We all must develop this ability more than ever before. In other words, present or perish!

Here are just a few of the reasons to improve your presentation skills:

1. Job promotions,
2. Raises,
3. More sales,
4. More productive meetings,
5. Less frustration and stress,
6. Stronger personal image, and
7. Better relationships.

Let's look at each of these reasons in detail.

Job promotions. Good jobs are at a premium. With companies and organizations downsizing and "rightsizing" more and more, desirable jobs are becoming more difficult to get. You can no longer walk into a personnel office, fill out an application, and get a job. You must be an aggressive marketer, and a major part of that marketing is presenting yourself.

Research shows that hiring decisions are based on 60 percent chemistry and 40% skills. In other words, managers hire and promote people they like and trust. You create chemistry with a person by the way you present yourself. Many people who look great on paper fail to convince managers to hire them.

If you have good presentation skills, you will get better jobs—because you'll be able to sell your skills by being a concise, organized, and enthusiastic presenter!

Raises. The higher you climb on the ladder of success, the more you'll be called upon to speak. You will have to convince upper management of your ideas. You'll have to motivate your staff. And you may have to represent your department, organization, or industry on panels or behind a podium.

More sales. Clearly, if you have good presentation and listening skills, you will increase your sales success. To be a good salesperson today, you must be an educator who can ask questions, understand needs, and organize information in a way that prospects can understand.

Top sales professionals know how to effectively present benefits to their listeners. They also know that selling is no longer a one-to-one affair. Salespeople must give seminars and demonstrations for large audiences in order to compete. That, of course, requires good presentation skills.

More productive meetings. Many meetings waste valuable time. But a meeting is nothing more than a presentation. To conduct an effective meeting, you must formulate a meaningful agenda, create interest, manage your time, answer questions, and provide specific action steps. These are the skills that all good presenters use—and you too can develop and use these skills.

Less frustration and stress. When you acquire and start using good presentation skills, you reduce frustration—yours and that of your audience members. Good presenters speak in a way that others can hear and understand. As a result, they get their message across clearly and increase their influence.

Stronger personal image. Image is important. Many promising people have lost jobs and promotions because they had a poor image when presenting.

Successful people know how to command an audience and project confidence. Companies and organizations often ask me to improve the presentation image of their employees, who are usually described as management material—bright and knowledgeable. But they're not dynamic presenters and they don't project confidence. Typically, their presentation skills are holding them back.

Better relationships. If you can express your ideas and feelings in a way that doesn't offend people, you'll be able to build better relationships. Knowing how to present from the listener's point of view is a critical skill. (We'll discuss this in Chapter 7.)

You've Got to Have Style

Good presenters are true to themselves. The goal of this book is to encourage you to find your true presentation style. If you're a quiet, easygoing type, you'll look ridiculous trying to be Tony Robbins, the dynamic, highly charged motivational speaker. If you're an expressive type, don't try to rein in all that energy! If you do, you'll lose your authenticity. Your greatest power as a

Exercise

Why do you need to improve your presentation skills? Check all the speaking situations that apply to you now or that will apply to you in the future. Rate your level of satisfaction for each area (needs significant improvement, needs some improvement, pretty good, and excellent).

	Needs significant improvement	Needs some improvement	Pretty good	Excellent
1. Formal standup speech				
2. Lead meetings				
3. Participate in meetings				
4. Interview for a job				
5. Sales call (one-to-one)				
6. Deliver seminars				
7. Teach a class (school/ community)				
8. Speak on the telephone				
9. Speak to customers				
10. Present dinner specials (restaurant)				
11. Provide technical support				
12. Give product demonstrations				
13. Interview on radio or TV				
14. Act in a play				
15. Train someone				
16 Issue a complaint				
17. Testify in court				
18 Mediate a dispute				
19. Give a sermon				
20. Deliver a keynote address				
21. Lead brainstorming				
22. Motivate a sports team				
23 Motivate a business team				
24. Raise funds				

25. Network (Yes, this is
      a presentation)
26. Give a public service
      announcement
27. Greet political constituents
28. Hold a press conference
29. Lead a question and
      answer session
30. Talk to patients
31. Other _____

Tally the number of checks in each column. You now have a good indication of how vital presentation skills are in your life. Even if you've checked nothing for now, things will likely change in the future.

presenter is to play to your strengths and be real.

At a training conference I once attended, the keynoter was a well-known consultant. He made fun of his own style, saying he wasn't dynamic.

He told the crowd that he didn't use enough gestures and that he'd been working on being dynamic for 30 years. From time to time he would use a gesture and remind us that he was doing so. By nature he was not dynamic. But he was a good speaker. He had something to say and he used humor to complement his laid-back style.

What is your natural style? As a presenter, are you dynamic?

Exercise

In a few words or a phrase, describe your presentation style:

_____

_____

authoritative? low-key? friendly? warm? sincere? funny?

The idea here is not to *judge* your presentation style, but to *identify* it. My style, for example, is high-energy, sincere, and inter-active. What's your style? If you're not sure, how would other people describe it? (If you don't know, ask them!)

It's important to know your presentation style so that you can capitalize on your strengths while you're speaking. Remember: your greatest power is to be real. There are thousands of speak-ers—but there is only one you!

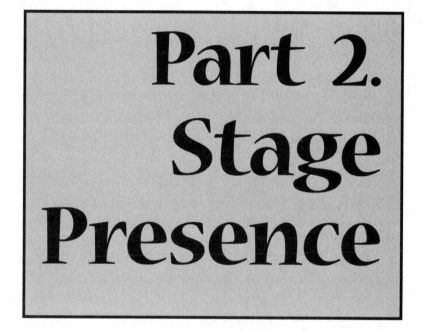

Part 2. Stage Presence

2

Sizzle or Steak?

You can't make it sing if it ain't got that swing.
–Duke Ellington

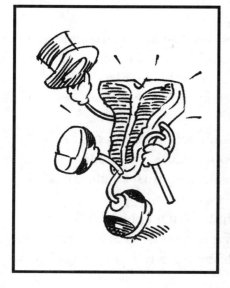

Sizzle or Steak:
An Ongoing Debate

What's more important—sizzle or steak? Style or substance? This is the ongoing debate about what makes a good speaker. The answer is, it depends.

Imagine receiving a beautifully wrapped package. It has expensive, colorful paper tied with shiny silver or gold bows. Each edge is perfectly creased. It calls out to you. It's almost too beautiful to open. The packaging is a work of art. Great image.

Now imagine that you open the gift. Inside is the hardcover book you've wanted. But the pages are yellow and worn. The outside cover is dark gray with no title. It has a scratch on the front. Some of the pages are missing. Even the story line is weak. Not much substance. Disappointing, isn't it?

You had high expectations based on the initial impression of the outside wrapping.

Suppose you see a box wrapped in plain brown paper with black lettering on the front. It's tied with re-used cord. Inside, however, unbeknownst to you, is the beautiful, silver Rolex watch you've long admired. Great value.

Chances are, you won't be much impressed with that package. It doesn't attract your attention. It has no presence. You're likely to discount it, even though it contains an object of real value.

You get the picture. Sizzle without steak is like eating chicken broth. It tastes good going down but it doesn't stay with you. An hour later you're probably hungry again. Steak without sizzle, on the other hand, is like eating mashed potatoes without gravy. It's substantive but not appetizing. It doesn't taste as good. Chances are you'll leave most of it on your plate.

So it is with speakers and audiences. The goal is to blend sizzle with steak. In this book, you'll learn how to be a dynamic presenter and how to develop substantive, well-organized content. But first you have to get people's attention.

So let's start with delivery.

In politics, sizzle and emotional appeal often win over substance. In business and, indeed, in politics, the best people have both. It's not enough to have the steak. You must be able to sell it with sizzle.

You may be saying, "Wait a minute. What about that boring CEO who gets all those speaking engagements?" As in other areas of life, there are always exceptions. There are two occasions when

The First Presidential Debate of 1996

Let's take a look at the first October 1996 presidential debate between Bob Dole and Bill Clinton. While the debate was close, most believed that Clinton had communicated his message more effectively. Dole was more energetic than usual, but he still needed to be more passionate about his message. His presentation was marked by rapid eye blinking and occasional stammering.

Although he used humor, Dole ended dispassionately. His call to "Just Do It" lacked emotional appeal, as did his invitation to visit his Web site. On a positive note, he used humor well and did not launch a strong personal attack against his opponent. Dole's biggest challenge was knowing how to sell his message and connect with the audience. He needed more sizzle before people would believe he had the steak.

Clinton's presentation was confident and polished. He connected with the audience by looking directly into the camera, using gestures, and exuding energy. He projected confidence, to the point that some people felt he was being slick.

Too much sizzle and you start sounding rehearsed. Not enough, and you'll bore your listeners.

Case Study

you can get away without sizzle:

- if you're a celebrity, or
- if you're a known expert.

A known expert is a respected specialist on a particular topic. People will come to hear such speakers because of the belief they will say something interesting or valuable. The expert may lack sparkle but the message has great value to the listeners. It's the data people want. This kind of speaker usually has a loyal following. Bill Gates is both an industry expert and a celebrity. People come to hear him because of his message and because of his name. He doesn't have to be entertaining.

Everything Is Communication

We're communicating all the time. Professor Albert Morabian of the Massachusetts Institute of Technology studied one-to-one social communication and discovered that communication happens on three levels:

- **Visual—55% (body language)**
- **Vocal—38% (tone of voice)**
- **Verbal—7% (words)**

By far, visual communication is the most powerful of the three types. People will believe body language over words. That's because your emotions are conveyed through your body. If your words and body language are inconsistent, people will believe what your body language says.

Dynamic speakers are congruent. That is, their body language, tone of voice, and words give the same message. When one of these is out of sync due to nervousness, the audience may question the speaker's credibility. So to be an effective speaker, you need to learn how to make sure your body language and words match one another.

The first presentation you'll make is the business handshake. There are three kinds of handshakes:

- the firm business handshake—a full clasp with some pressure,
- the vise grip—a bone-crushing grasp (a problem if you are wearing a ring!), and
- the jelly fish—the hand just hangs there.

People have lost job opportunities, promotions, customers, and relationships because of something so minor as a handshake. One trading manager of a New York investment banking firm confided, "I never hire a person with a weak handshake."

Is this fair? No. But it's reality. A limp handshake communicates weakness, indecisiveness, lack of conviction. A crushing handshake communicates aggressiveness, power plays, and maybe even intimidation.

To be an effective presenter, you need to get off to a good start by greeting others with a firm handshake and direct eye contact. (More about eye contact later.)

Let's continue to observe how the body communicates in subtle and not so subtle ways.

Let Me Hear Your Body Talk

There are many ways the body communicates. Here are some examples of what some actions can mean:

- *Rapid eye blinking*. When you see someone's eyes blinking rapidly, more than eight to ten times per minute, chances are the person disagrees with you.
- *Dilated pupils*. Pupils that are open suggest interest.
- *"Steepling" fingers*. This is usually a sign of power. People who want to project authority will often steeple their hands by putting them together with only the fingertips touching.
- *Clenched fists*. Clenched hands can indicate frustration.
- *Folded arms.*When people fold their arms in front or in back, they may be protecting themselves. They might also be defensive—or even chilly!
- *Hands touching mouth or nose*. This could be a signal that the person is lying.
- *Raised eyebrow*. Raised eyebrows usually mean surprise.
- *Tilting head forward*. Leaning toward the speaker shows interest. It means the listener is tuned in. When the hand is supporting the head, the listener is usually bored.
- *Leaning away*. This posture can mean disagreement or lack of interest. If the listener suddenly leans back, change the subject or direction of the conversation.
- *Drumming fingers*. This gesture could mean frustration or irritation.

First Impressions

People are always making judgments about each other. It takes seven seconds or less to make your first impression. If that impression is negative, it's difficult to turn it around.

Similarly, you'll be judged as a speaker from the moment you walk into the room. That means your presentation begins before you ever open your mouth. To create a positive impression, you need to master how to take and leave the platform.

Most speakers simply approach the podium and launch into their presentation: "Good morning. My name is Susie Speaker and I'm here to talk about…" Stop! Settle down. The audience is not ready to hear you. Before you start presenting, scan the audience and:

- Breathe,
- Collect your thoughts,
- Receive the audience,
- Take the listeners in,
- Feel the energy coming toward you,
- Say, "Good morning/afternoon/evening," and
- Pause long enough for people to respond.

Then you can begin your opening remarks. By having a smooth walk on, you create a relationship with the audience.

The same thought process applies to ending your presentation. Many speakers simply hurry off the platform following the presentation. They thank the audience and rush away, rolling their eyes as if to say, "Thank God it's over." And in doing so, they sabotage themselves.

At the end of your presentation, pause and accept the audience's approval. Applause is a gift. To rush off stage is to reject that gift. Smile and soak it in. Then walk off with confidence. That's presence.

Practice this activity, called "walk-on/walk-off," with a small group.
1. Get up from your seat and approach the front of the room.
2. Breathe.
3 Look out at the audience. Connect with them through the eyes.
4. Say, "Good morning." Pause and wait for people to respond. "My name is...."
5. The group will then clap. Stay there and receive the applause.
6. Walk confidently to your seat. (If you roll your eyes, you must start all over again.)

Exercise

Acts of Sabotage

If the audience is watching you squirm, they're not listening. You can easily distract the audience by little acts of self-sabotage.

These detracting behaviors can be visual, vocal, or verbal—the audience can focus on what they see you do with your body, what they hear in your voice, or the inappropriate words and filler sounds you use (such as "uh," "um," and others). When the audience begins to notice nervous behaviors, they start to lose your message. But you have a message you want to get across.

In this segment we'll identify the most common nervous behaviors speakers display and what you can do about them. Since body language is most powerful, let's start by examining the most common problem—visual sabotage.

Visual Sabotage

Pacing back and forth. Rocking and rolling. Few or no gestures. Fidgety fingers. Inappropriate appearance. Little or no eye contact. If you engage in any of these behaviors when presenting, don't worry. They're easy to fix. Here are some simple steps you can take.

Feet. *Find your "power center."* Your power center is from the waist

Exercise

Stand on a piece of aluminum foil about two feet long. Every time you shift from foot to foot you will hear a crinkly sound. This will remind you to stop swaying and to use hand gestures instead.

up. Powerful speakers concentrate their energy from the waist to the face.

Stay planted. Anchor your feet and stand up straight. Leaning or slouching indicates a lack of confidence or conviction. There is no power in your feet. If you pace back and forth, you signal that your nervousness is in your feet. Once you're planted, put your energy into your hands. If you start rocking back and forth, you'll look like a human metronome and the audience will fall asleep.

Move with purpose. The most dynamic speakers move, but they always have a good reason for doing so. Work the room by moving into the center of the audience. Walk over to another side of the room. Stand there and deliver a new point. This purposeful movement looks confident and focused.

Exercise

Stand on the floor. Take three 8 1/2-inch by 11-inch sheets of paper. Put one sheet on the floor four feet in front of you. Take another sheet and place it three feet to the right of where you're standing. Place the third sheet three feet to the left of where you're standing. Now begin speaking and move toward one of the papers. Step on the paper and make your point. Stay there until you're ready to change topics. Walk over slowly to another sheet and speak to your audience. No, you are not doing the cha-cha. You are moving with purpose.

Hands. *Talk with your hands.* Yes, that's right. Forget what your teachers told you. Effective speakers express themselves with their hands. Nervous presenters lock their hands in front of themselves. This is called the "fig leaf" position. Other speakers lock their arms behind them until the audience wonders if the speaker has hands.

Don't contain your energy! You'll only look stiff and more nervous. Fidgeting is a scream for help. Your hands are saying, "I WANT TO MOVE!" When you hold back the energy, it leaks out in little unwanted fidgets. So don't resist. Give in to the natural energy that your hands want to express.

Get excited about your message and your hands will move by themselves. If you're really not natural with gestures, try bringing your hands waist high. Gestures that are above the waist make you look confident. (Remember the power center.) Hand movements below the waist look weak or tentative.

Another option is to use your hands to count off. List the agenda items or objectives of your talk. As you speak, tick off each item on your fingers. You can also paint pictures with gestures. Describe an object or process by moving your hands. Interacting with a chart or screen is another way to use your hands effectively. Touch the visual as you make your point.

Caution: Do not plan your gestures. Some speakers mark up their notes, calculating which gesture to use with which word. They end up looking robotic. Strive to be natural.

- Select a group of antonyms—big-small, high-low, narrow-wide, up-down, flat-curved, open-closed. As you say the words, make the appropriate gestures with your hands.
- Tell a story about a vacation or sport. As you tell the story, act it out with your hands. Exaggerate the hand movements. Storytelling is one of the best ways to learn how to use gestures.

Exercise

Appearance. *Look the part.* Is image important? You bet it is! How you look communicates volumes to the listeners. Dress appropriately for the presentation. That means doing your homework. Is it a formal audience? Dress for success. In other words, wear stylish, well-fitting clothes that don't call attention to yourself, yet still look good on you.

Are you addressing people from the factory floor? Throw away the three-piece suit. Casual dress is in order. If you're speaking to bankers, don't wear that flashy number. They'll respect a more conservative image.

Here are some do's and don'ts for dressing to speak:

WOMEN	**MEN**
No heavy make-up	Button jacket
Business suit or dress	White or neutral shirt
No micro-mini skirts	Wear dark suits
Conservative hairstyles	Straighten tie
No jangling jewelry	No pens in pockets
Avoid brightly colored	No flashy belt buckles
or textured hose	Dark socks to match suit
No revealing necklines	Polished shoes
Wear a comfortable garment	Avoid tinted glasses
Don't buy a new outfit	Wear calf-length socks

Here's the best advice: Check yourself in a full length mirror before the presentation.

Consider these factors when dressing to speak:

Geography. Will it be warm or cold where you're going? If you're traveling in winter from New York to Florida, the wool tweed suit won't do. Be sensitive to regional differences and dress accordingly. The Northeast is more sophisticated and formal than are other parts of the country. Women wear fewer suits in the South.

If you're speaking overseas, follow the guidelines of that country. Keep in mind that in certain countries it is inappropriate for women to wear pants suits or to bear their arms.

If you travel frequently, look for fabrics that don't require a lot of care. A silk or wool blend is a good choice. Carry suits in a separate garment bag to minimize wrinkling. You can purchase a portable steamer or hang the garment near a hot shower to remove wrinkles.

Case Study

The Networking Meeting

Several years ago, I wanted to make a career change. I had the opportunity to meet with someone in my chosen field. Usually I would go to the restroom before such a meeting, but when I arrived, my contact was standing at the door.

So I shook hands and he escorted me to his office. I decided to forgo my usual trip to the restroom. How much disarray could take place walking from the coffee shop to the office building?

I gave what I thought was a good presentation. When I left the building, I caught a glimpse of my reflection in a store window. I noticed a smudge on my face. As I stared at my reflection, I rubbed at my face wondering what this could be. Then I realized the shocking truth: It was chocolate! (I had eaten David's Cookies before the interview.) My host had let me sit there with chocolate on my face without telling me. Luckily, I never saw him again.

Moral: Never present yourself without first checking your appearance in a mirror.

Organizational culture. Certain organizations have a distinct uniform. The clothes worn by people in these organizations create an image as recognizable as the organization's logo. If you speak at IBM, you'll want the conservative, pin-stripe suit. If you speak for the fashion industry, forget conservative. Wear this year's color and style with tasteful accessories. Do your homework. Look at photos in annual reports. Ask people who know the culture. Go on-site if possible. Stand in the lobby and observe how people dress. For your own organization, follow the dress code. When in doubt, err on the side of being formal and conservative.

Audience and circumstances. What group and level will you be addressing? If you're addressing clerical workers and you look like you just stepped off of a fashion runway, you may appear intimidating. Will you be speaking to an international audience? Will it be a women's conference? Are you speaking at a trade show and invited to the company dinner that evening? Is the audience composed of conservative businessmen? Are you speaking to high school students? What is the setting? Is it at a convention of 500 or will you speak to a group of twenty?

Do your homework when speaking abroad. In China, if a woman wears red, she may be perceived as arrogant or wanting to stand out. Check with cultural experts and dress appropriately for the country.

Quality of clothing. They say that clothes make the man or woman. Your clothes talk. They can make the sale and they definitely make an impression. They signal your social status, economic status, personal style, industry, and job level. Many people are passed over for promotions because they don't look the part. You'll even receive a different quality of service based on how you're dressed.

Next time you're in a restaurant, watch who gets the table by the kitchen. Not the person who's dressed to the nines. This is especially true in image-type businesses. One advertising executive notices shoes. He can judge how successful vendors are by the quality of their shoes. If you have a limited budget, invest in one good-quality suit for speaking occasions. Look for a reputable label and a natural fabric. Be sure it fits well by investing in a good tailor as well.

Color of clothing. Gray, black, navy, and brown are conservative business colors. Women have more options than men. Red and royal purple can be power colors. A bright color signals that you want to be noticed.

According to Carolyn Gustafson, a New York City image consultant, red can be tiring to the eye. For an all-day presentation, red may not be the best choice. Instead, Gustafson recommends burgundy. Burgundy has the positive, high-vitality energy of red without the fatigue factor. Another good choice is royal blue. Gustafson calls it the "Sarah Lee of blue. Nobody doesn't like royal blue."

Color is friendly. When I teach presentation skills, I don't wear black. It's too intimidating and people are already nervous. Avoid the color green. It does not suggest power. It conveys nurturing. To be perceived as authoritative, choose darker colors and avoid pastels. Men especially should not wear brown. They will lose the image of authority.

Accessories. *Make sure that your shoes, socks, and belts are the same color.* Wear brown accessories with a brown suit. You can wear black accessories with any other color. Keep your accessories minimal. For women, a strand of pearls or a silk scarf can accent an outfit. Avoid loud patterns in scarves and ties.

If the audience is focused on your attire, they're not listening. One woman in my seminar was working on being more dynamic. She learned to use expansive gestures. The only problem was she had very long, bright red fingernails. Every time she gestured people were riveted by her red fingertips!

Here's a way to manage your image using the squint test. Image consultant Carolyn Gustafson recommends standing back, squinting your eyes, and looking in the mirror. What do you notice? Is there anything that stands out or distracts? If so, remove it. Don't let your appearance compete with your presentation.

Exercise

Eyes. *Connect with your eyes.* Eye contact is a critical platform skill. In U.S. culture, we don't trust people who avert their eyes from ours. We say they're lying, untrustworthy, trying to hide something. To be perceived as sincere, look into people's eyes. But don't stare—just look long enough to complete a thought.

Find a friendly face and speak to that person. In other words, don't talk to the crowd, talk to individuals. It's not hard. For large audiences, divide the room into quadrants. Start with one of these quadrants and talk to one person there for three to five seconds. Look at and talk to someone toward the back for a sentence or two. Continue speaking to one person at a time in different quadrants of the room. The people in that section will think you're looking directly at them. This enables you to achieve balance with all parts of the room.

Don't look down at the floor or up at the ceiling. You may be thinking, but your audience will not perceive you as thoughtful. They'll view you as lacking in confidence. Even if you lose your train of thought, don't look away. Keep the connection. By holding a person's gaze and pausing, you will better conceal the fact that you're collecting your thoughts. It will look like a dramatic pause.

Exercise

1. At home, set up a couple of rows of chairs. Have four friends act as your audience.
2. Put each person in a corner chair. Begin talking about a topic.
3. Each person will raise a hand for five seconds. Your job is to make eye contact with each person for five seconds. Have each person count silently (one-one thousand, two-one thousand, three-one thousand, four-one thousand, five-one thousand). If you break contact, have that person wave his or her hand.
4. If you've maintained eye contact without looking away, the person's hand will drop, and you can go on to the next person.
5. Look at the next person for five seconds while speaking. When his or her hand drops, begin looking at the next person.
6. Now transfer that skill to a large audience.

Variation: You don't have any friends who can come over? You're not off the hook. Place stuffed animals in the chairs and practice the above exercise. The goal is to practice eye contact, not to have a conversation. I've done this myself and it really works. The down side is that my husband now thinks I like to talk to teddy bears. Don't worry about it. It works.

Vocal Sabotage

Now let's look at the ways your voice can undermine your ability to present effectively. There are many ways you can hurt yourself here, but they all have cures:

- Non-words,
- Volume,
- Speaking rate,
- Monotone,
- Rising inflection (uptalk),
- Losing your train of thought (going blank),
- Being canned (talking head), and
- Vocal problems (nasal, hoarse, high-pitch, breath).

Here are some ways for dealing with each of these problems.

Non-words. *Pause.* The "ahs" have it. Non-words are fillers—um, ah, you know, like, OK, basically. When you pepper your speech with such words and fillers, you lose credibility. Any word, sentence, or gesture that you repeat so often that people start counting qualifies as a non-word.

Speakers um and ah because they're afraid of silence. The remedy is to pause. Pausing will give you the thinking time you need. Your audience will perceive the pause as confidence.

Volume. *Vary your volume and breathe deeply.* Volume can detract from your message in two ways: if it is inappropriate for the situation or if you speak at a single volume.

Are you booming at a handful of people? Do people back away from you? If so, learn to vary your voice. Experiment. Increase your volume to generate excitement and speak more softly to create intimacy. (Note: If people complain that your speech is normally too loud, you may have a hearing loss. Get a checkup.)

More often speakers are too soft. If your voice is barely audible, it may be that you're simply shy. It could also be the result of improper breathing. A breathy voice may sound sexy on the

Exercise

To stop using non-words, get a friend to help.
1. Choose a subject you know well—for instance, how to ski, how you get ready in the morning, or how to bake a cake.
2. Start talking.
3. Ask your friend to snap his or her fingers every time you say an um or ah.
4. Eventually, you'll anticipate the snaps and stop yourself.

Variation: You don't have a friend handy? Place a rubber band around your wrist. Give a short speech into a tape recorder. Then, listen to the recording and snap the rubber band every time you hear a non-word. Next, play the tape again and count the ums and other non-words. Repeat the exercise until you reduce the number of non-words you use.

Next step: Keep the rubber band on and make a phone call. Give a light snap when you hear an um—either from you or the person you're talking to.

phone, but it's weak and inefficient on the platform. Practice breathing deeply so air fills your chest. (See Chapter 3 on controlling nervousness.) If you're speaking to a large group, request a microphone.

Exercise

1. Stand one foot away from a friend.
2. Have your friend extend his or her arm toward you, with the palm facing you as if signaling you to stop.
3. Take in a deep breath.
4. Say your name. "Hello, my name is Sam Speaker." Try to hit your friend's hand with your voice.
5. Have your friend step back another two feet. Say the same sentence and try hitting the palm with your voice.
6. Continue doing this exercise in intervals of two feet until you have to project your voice twenty feet.
7. Notice how your projection has improved.

Speaking rate. *Slow down and pause.* Are you a speed demon? Most people think that the faster they speak, the sooner they can sit down. The trouble is, if you rush through your presentation, your audience won't absorb your message. And if you speak really fast, the audience will stop listening altogether. So slow down. Pause. The brain needs a few seconds to process information. By pausing, you help the audience listen.

Monotone. *Move your hands and find your passion.* Do you suffer from insomnia? Here's a quick cure. Listen to a monotone speaker. A monotone is a flat, lifeless voice with no highs or lows. It happens for two reasons. The speaker may truly lack conviction and enthusiasm. More often, however, the speaker is simply nervous.

If you tend to present with a monotone voice, try using more gestures. There is a relationship between your hands and your voice. By moving your hands you increase your energy. That energy will then come through in your voice.

Mark up your notes. Underline key words with a red pencil. Emphasize those words by raising your voice.

You can also use your voice to vary the meaning of what you're saying. Practice these sentences. Emphasize the italicized word to change the message:
- *I* didn't say you stole money.
- I *didn't* say you stole money.
- I didn't *say* you stole money.
- I didn't say *you* stole money.
- I didn't say you *stole* money.
- I didn't say you stole *money*.

If you have a serious case of monotone, practice singing your message. Doing so will create varying intonation in your voice. After doing this, try speaking your message once again. You'll notice a difference.

Most important, find your passion. What excites you about this topic? If it's a technical talk, include stories and examples that

Case Study

> ### President John F. Kennedy
> President Kennedy was regarded as a good speaker. But he didn't start out that way. During the early years, he spoke in a fast-paced monotone. People could not process what he was saying because he rarely paused.
>
> He did one thing to change himself. According to his secretary, Evelyn Lincoln, Kennedy started talking on only one topic: the presidency. He found his passion. All of his other speeches were subcategories of the presidency. With this major topic and his newly found passion, Kennedy was able to speak with a level of conviction that elevated him as a speaker. It was his enthusiasm for the topic that helped him become a memorable speaker.

excite you and that bring the presentation to life. To help in this, do the hub and spoke exercise.

Exercise

> What is your main topic or area of expertise? Think of this area as the hub of a wheel. Now what are your subtopics? These are the spokes of the wheel. Look at the example in Figure 2-1 (page 37).
>
> Then fill in the hub of Figure 2-2 with your main presentation topic. Now fill in the spokes. What subtopics could be speeches? You'll notice that your expertise tends to fall into a general category. Perhaps that general category is technology or finance. Ask yourself, what is it that I speak about on a regular basis? What do people most often ask me about? What are my most requested speech topics? Which aspects of these topics most excite me? These are the topics you can develop a passion about.

Rising inflection. *Tape yourself.* A speaker's intonation should go up at the end of a sentence only when he or she is asking a question. If your presentation is filled with rising inflections, you'll sound tentative and unsure of yourself. Are you asking permission or are you speaking with conviction?

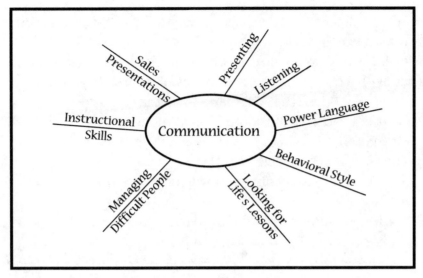

Figure 2-1. Hub and spokes: Communication

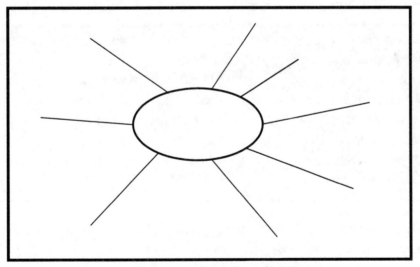

Figure 2-2. Create your own hub-and-spoke diagram

Losing your train of thought. *Familiarize; don't memorize.* Going blank during your presentation could be a sign of aging, but that's not likely. Speakers who lose their train of thought during speeches usually have memorization fever, like the actor who memorizes lines. Stop it! Study key concepts instead of words. Then if you go

Exercise

Read the following sentences. Put a downward arrow at the end of each sentence. Speak into a tape recorder. Read each section with a rising inflection (as if you're asking a question). Then read each sentence with a downward inflection. Now listen to the recording.

1. We are confident that the market will turn around.
2. I expect to achieve my quota by next month.
3. My manager invests in my professional development.
4. The team is experiencing conflict.
5. After the initial screening, you will meet with the hiring manager.

   Notice the difference in the way you sound—and in how you might be perceived by audience members?

blank, you can say it a different way. The audience will never know the difference.

Exercise

Have a plan for recovering from those situations when you suddenly go blank. You can recap the point you just made. Or, you can pose a question to the audience: "At this point I'd like to get your opinion on what I just proposed." You can also pause, look for your place, and move on. The audience will wait; they won't get up and leave. If you're really stuck, ask the audience to help you out. If you say, "Where was I?" someone will remind you. People are human. You don't have to be perfect.

Being canned. *Have a conversation.* You've heard canned talks. They often happen at dinner time—when the phone rings. "Hello, Ms. Jones. How are you tonight? We at XYZ company have a special program we'd like to tell you about... blah, blah, blah." You know the person on the other end is reading word for word. Don't be a talking head. A canned speech sounds contrived and artificial. Practice being conversational and spontaneous. Good speakers are present in the moment. What's most important is

Exercise

Review your notes and convert them to bullet points. Then, sit down. (This will eliminate some of the formality you're feeling.) In your own words, review each point out loud. Have a conversation. Try saying things in different ways. You should not sound scripted. If a new thought pops up, go with it. Spontaneity is a strength.

making a connection with your listeners. Sincerity sells.

Vocal problems. *It's all in the voice.* A distinctive voice like James Earl Jones' can be very attractive and memorable. A distinctive voice like Fran Drescher's nasal whine can distract the audience from your message.

Voices can be too nasal, too hoarse, too high-pitched, or too breathy. A nasal voice actually lacks nasal resonance. Pinch your nostrils, and you'll experience the nasal voice.

Exercise

To add resonance to your voice, do these activities:
1. Hum.
2. Place two fingers on the side of your nose. Feel the vibration when you speak. Now feel the vibrations on top of your head. Maybe you didn't know there were vibrations, but there are.
3. Practice this word list and feel your nose and the top of your head for vibration.
   man, can, fan, tan, ran, ban, pan, ann, dan, fran, van
   hand, band, land, sand, bland, gland, brand, grand,
   jam, lamb, sam, ham, dam, wam, pam, ram, tram
   sing, ring, king, ding, thing, ming, wing, zing

A hoarse voice sounds raspy. Hoarseness may be due to laryngitis. Or it may be a case of vocal abuse, such as shouting, straining, or overuse. In these situations, the remedy is vocal rest and training on how to properly use the voice . Don't make phone calls for a day. Rest on the weekends. In some cases, a chronic hoarse voice is a symptom of throat nodules. These calluses or growths can be reduced with speech therapy. See a physician for a vocal checkup if your voice is continually sore.

A high-pitched voice can be irritating to listen to. It can also rob you of authority during your presentation. To find your natural pitch, you can do several things:

1. Sigh.
2. Say, "Uh huh."
3. Sigh out, "Uh huh." (This is your natural pitch)

You can also "count down." Go down to your lowest pitch possible. Say "do re mi fa sol..." as you go up in pitch. By the time you reach sol, you'll be at your natural pitch.

Breathiness is more common in women than in men. Many men and women think a breathy voice sounds sexy, but it's the least efficient voice there is. Breathiness occurs because there is an extra escapage of air while speaking. To correct this problem:

1. Practice diaphragmatic breathing. (Do this by taking deep breaths that make your chest expand.)
2. Tape your voice and listen for breathiness. Say the same sentence several times by first taking in enough air and then projecting your voice. Begin with short sentences and work up to longer sentences. (The longer sentences take more breath to speak, and if there is a breathiness it may be more apparent with longer sentences.) If you have a severe case of breathiness, consider working with a voice coach.

Verbal Sabotage

There are many words and phrases that can sabotage your speech. Among them:
- Taglines,
- Wimpy words,
- Jargon,
- Apologies,

- Minimizers,
- Colorless words, and
- Sloppy speech.

You've already learned that non-verbal communication (body language and voice) is about 90% of your message. So how can words have much impact?

Words are powerful! Have you ever read a Stephen King thriller or a romance novel? How were you able to feel such fear and suspense or romance and passion? It was the power of the words. Words can dampen and deter or excite and motivate. Hypnotists put people into trances with their words.

So how do words get in the way? A study published in the *Journal of the International Listening Association* demonstrated that speakers using "powerless" language were considered less competent and less credible when evaluated by their listeners. "Powerless" language was defined as containing non-words ("um," "you know"), taglines ("This is a good idea, don't you think?"), and wimpy words ("I think," "I guess").

Taglines. *Eliminate them.* If you use taglines such as "Don't you think?" "Isn't it?" or "Right?" you'll weaken your conviction. Do you believe what you're saying? Then don't ask permission. The audience will not be convinced unless you are.

Wimpy words. *Substitute power words.* Wimpy words are another credibility killer. A wimpy word weakens your message and makes you appear tentative. Listen to the difference in these two statements:

> *"**Hopefully**, I've **tried** to show you that this is **kind of** a good product, and maybe **if** you'll try it you'll be convinced."*

Convinced? With such tentative language, not likely.

Take two. Let's delete the wimpy words and express this confidently:

> *"I've demonstrated how effectively this product can meet your needs. I am confident that when you use it you'll be convinced."*

Which speaker would you listen to? Many otherwise good ideas are lost because the speaker didn't know how to present them with confidence.

Exercise

> Say these words aloud. How do you feel when you say wimpy words as opposed to power words?
>
> | **Wimpy Words** | **Power Words** |
> | --- | --- |
> | I feel | I know |
> | I believe | I am confident |
> | If | When, By |
> | Suggest | Recommend |
> | Sort of/Kind of | It is |
> | Might/Perhaps | Definitely/Absolutely |
> | I hope | I know |
> | May | Can |
> | Worried | Concerned |
> | Problem | Challenge |
> | I'll try | I will/I'm committed |
> | Share | Discuss |
>
> Wimpy words usually will project that you are unsure and unwilling to make a commitment. Power words project confidence and assure people.

Jargon. *Spell it out.* Jargon is another detractor. When you add acronyms and buzzwords to your presentation, you risk losing part or all of the audience.

Assume that nobody understands your "business speak." Always define the entire term or phrase first. Later on you can refer to the acronym. For example: "As we implement management by objective, or MBO...."

Look over your notes and delete jargon. Substitute language that everyone can understand. Remember: your goal is to make the message clear.

Apologies. *Skip them.* Don't apologize or put yourself down. Audience members will interpret this as a sign of weakness. "Sorry" or "excuse me" are appropriate when you've done something wrong. There's no reason to tell the audience that you're nervous or that you feel unprepared.

Minimizers. *Delete them.* Minimizers are words such as "just" and "only." *I just got lucky. I'm only a beginner.* These words have a negative connotation. What's wrong with being a beginner? We all have to start somewhere. Minimizers tell the listener that you're less than something. Delete them from your vocabulary. Don't minimize yourself or your message.

Tape a five-minute presentation. Then, listen to the tape and write down any wimpy words, taglines, or jargon you hear. Eliminate the taglines and substitute power words. Now listen again for non-words. Count them. We all use one or two. If you have more than one um per minute, try the rubber band technique on page 34.

Wimpy Words   Taglines   Non-words   Minimizers

Shortcut: Ask a friend or colleague if you use any of the verbal detractors described above. Set a goal to eliminate them from your speech.

Exercise

Colorless words. *Paint a word picture.* Colorless words are dull, lackluster, matter-of-fact words that don't create much reaction in the listener. Good speakers use vivid language. Vivid language adds color to your speech and helps the listener create pictures from your words. In the following example, which sentence is more vivid and descriptive?

1. If you make your presentation fun, the audience will accept you.

2. The audience members will cradle you in the arms of approval if they're having fun.

Pepper your talk with colorful language. Use metaphors, analogies, alliteration, and onomatopoeia.

Metaphor: He was a lion in battle.

Analogy: Think of a speech as a sandwich. The pieces of bread are the opening and closing. The thickest part is the meat in the middle. Save the details for the meat of the speech.

Alliteration: Be concise, clear, and confident.

Onomatopoeia: Snap, crackle, pop.

Sloppy speech. *Speak slowly and carefully.* Mumbling, mispronunciations, and slurred speech create a negative impression and are difficult to understand. We can define sloppy speech as vague, ambiguous, and filled with clichés. Sloppy speech leaves people unsure of your message. This kind of speech pattern corrupts your message and creates an impression that you are uneducated or lacking credibility.

When your speech is unclear, it's usually a result of one of the following problems: omissions, substitutions, distortions, or additions.

- An omission is the elimination of a sound or syllable: "stree" for "street" or "rithmetic" for "arithmetic."
- A substitution is a word that contains the wrong sound used for the correct sound, as in "wif" for "with" or "shair" for "chair."
- A distortion occurs when the speaker pronounces a sound incorrectly. An example would be a lateral emission lisp, in which a person producing the "s" sound releases air from the sides of the mouth instead of directing it through the front of the mouth. This articulation results in a sloppy sounding "s." Carol Channing has this distortion. While it has almost become a trademark for her, remember what we said about celebrities: they can get away with more.

> ### Sloppy Speech
>
> Recently I saw a medical expert on the television news. She was an M.D. and had the credentials to speak about health. However, she lost credibility because of her articulation. She would mispronounce words—for example, she said "thurpy" for "therapy" and "aks" for "ask." They were distracting, and I found myself questioning whether she was really an M.D. Her speech was not consistent with her knowledge and educational credentials. If I was noticing this, it's likely that other listeners were distracted as well. Is your diction consistent with your education and position?

Case Study

- An addition occurs when the speaker adds an extra syllable to a word, as in the case of "ath-a-lete" for "athlete."

The key to changing them is awareness and practice. I'm not suggesting there is anything wrong with regionalisms. It's just that they can distract people from hearing your message.

Sloppy speech patterns may result from bad habits, but they may also appear for physical reasons. If you have any of these patterns, get a hearing checkup. A hearing loss can affect your speech. If you slur your speech because you speak too rapidly, follow the exercises for slowing down and pausing.

There could also be structural reasons behind your inability to enunciate clearly. The articulators are the tongue, teeth, lips, gums, jaw, hard palate, soft palate, and larynx. When one of these is not working effectively, the clarity of your speech can be affected. A visit to a speech therapist will help you determine the cause of the problem and develop a program of remediation. Another alternative is to take a voice and diction class. Many local colleges and acting schools offer such courses.

We've examined the most common presentation mistakes that can detract from your message. Now you have some easy, clear-cut techniques and strategies to help you avoid these mistakes and work on any weakness you have that might lead to them.

Exercise

Practice the plosive sounds. Plosives are sounds in which the air stream is blocked and then released or exploded with a burst of energy. Plosives are also referred to as "stops" because the air is stopped completely. There are six plosive sounds: p as in pie, b as in buy, t as in tie, d as in dye, k as in key, and g as in guy. By practicing plosive sounds, you'll add crispness to your speech. Tongue twisters are especially good material for practicing these speech sounds.

Say the following sentences aloud:
- Pete passed the mashed potatoes and pot pie.
- Please pick up the papers and pile them.
- Upon the pavement, Patsy pushed the pink wheels of her apple cart.

- Betty blurted, "Be the best."
- Burt bought somebody a barbecued burger.
- Ben boasted that the buds bloomed on his birthday

- Two plus ten plus ten count up to twenty-two.
- Ted Thompson was told to take the table to the left.
- Terry told the tailor not to tighten the waist.

- Dan described the lady as he fell into a deep sleep.
- Do you like to dance until dawn?
- Deliver the desk by midnight to the doorman on Dean Street.

- Kathy kept her broken cane next to the black kettle.
- Kramer came to a keen conclusion that the Correggio was a fake.
- Keep the closet door closed or the kitten will claw the clothes.

- Go get a good keg of grape juice.
- Gary grabbed the egg salad and gave the meager leftovers to Gail.
- Maggie gained a good reputation for baking good goose.

But I know what you're thinking—"I'm still nervous." No problem. Turn to Chapter 3, where we will discuss ways that you can conquer your nervousness.

Checklist for Visual Delivery Skills

DO

- **Eliminate distracting behaviors**. Videotape yourself and listen to your delivery. Then, turn down the sound and watch your body language. Identify any behaviors that get in the way of your message. If your audience is concentrating on your movements or habits, they have stopped listening. Substitute positive behaviors.
- **Be real**. Audiences are more sophisticated than ever. They see through phoniness. Be genuine and capitalize on your strengths. If you're low-key, don't try to be frenetic. Enhance your own style instead of imitating someone else's. Speak from your heart and tell your own story. Embrace silence. Allow time for your words and message to sink in.
- **Extend eye contact**. Look directly at people in the audience for a complete sentence or two. This takes five seconds or less. In a large auditorium, break the room into three or four sections. Start with the corners of the room. Look at a person for five seconds, then move on to someone in another section for five seconds. Continue to do this until you've connected with all sections of the audience.
- **Expand your gestures**. The lack of gestures can make a speaker look stiff. Gestures that are close to the body can have the same effect. Use your hands to paint a picture, to count off agenda items, or to point to a visual aid. Get involved in your message and your hands will move naturally. Enthusiasm can be seen in the hands and heard in the voice.
- **Stand up straight**. A slumping posture will create a negative

impression. When you stand up straight, you increase your personal presence and allow yourself to breathe properly.

- **Move with purpose**. Rocking and rolling or pacing will distract your audience. Plant your feet and put your energy into making gestures. If you can't stay still, try moving with purpose. Walk into the audience and talk to one person. After you make your point, move toward someone else and talk to him or her. You'll burn off nervous energy while looking confident and dynamic.
- **Be enthusiastic**. Get excited about your talk. Don't be afraid to be animated and expressive. Increase your energy through movement and facial expression. Smile! Remember: enthusiasm is contagious.

DON'T

- **Play with a pen or a pointer**. This distraction signals that you're nervous. Use a pen to write, then put it down.
- **Turn your back on the audience**. We connect through the eyes. Learn to walk backward instead of turning your back.

Checklist for Vocal Delivery Skills

DO

- **Listen to your voice**. Tape yourself when you're rehearsing, giving a speech, using a microphone, or on the telephone. Evaluate yourself for pitch, pace, personality, and pleasantness.
- **Vary your intonation**. The highs and lows in your voice add color, excitement, and interest. Practice with a pitch pipe or by playing scales on a piano. Work on emphasizing a different word in the same sentence.
- **Reflect enthusiasm and passion**. Get excited about your message. If you're excited, it will come through in your voice. The voice, like body language, reflects the unconscious. If you

don't believe what you're saying, your voice will betray you. If you can't feel passionate about your message, find another topic.

- **Experiment with volume**. A well-timed whisper or burst of volume may add the dramatic effect you need to make a point and stimulate audience interest.
- **Project**. Talk to the back rows. Stand up straight, with your head up. Imagine hitting the back wall with your voice. Use your abdominal muscles and diaphragm to supply the power.
- **Speak with optimum pitch**. A pitch that is too high or too low will cause strain on your voice. To find your optimum pitch, use the "uh huh" method. Say "uh huh" a couple of times. The pitch you use to hum "uh huh" is your optimum or natural pitch.
- **Eliminate negative vocal qualities**. Be honest. Are you raspy like Marlon Brando in *The Godfather*? Do you squeak like Mickey Mouse? It may be time to get some vocal training. A hoarse or nasal voice can be distracting to the listener and damaging to your vocal cords.
- **Put a smile in your voice**. A happy-sounding, pleasant voice is engaging and warm. People can actually sense a smile over the phone. So practice smiling as you speak.
- **Take in enough air**. Gasping for air causes you to rush and sound nervous when you're speaking. Breathe deeply and parcel out enough air to finish the sentence.

DON'T

- **Drink ice water**. Room-temperature water with lemon is the best choice for speakers. Ice water can cause constriction of the vocal folds.
- **Drink alcohol, coffee, or milk products**. Avoid these beverages before you speak. Alcohol is a depressant and may loosen your inhibitions too much. The caffeine in coffee will make you feel jittery. Milk products create mucus, which will force

you to have to clear your throat frequently.

- **Continually clear your throat**. This causes damage to your vocal folds over time. Swallow instead.
- **Speak over loud music or noise**. This will cause you to strain and harm your voice.
- **Yell**. If you have to shout to get the crowd's attention, bang on a glass, blow a whistle, play music, or designate someone else to call the audience to order.

Checklist for Verbal Delivery Skills

DO

- **Use specific, precise language**. Speaking is impaired by vague terminology. Words like "some" and "a lot" don't say much and won't convince your audience to take action. "We can increase our membership by 60% in two years" is clear and measurable. Generalities are weak and confusing. The power to persuade lies in specific language.
- **Use vivid language**. Paint a picture to give color to your speech. Contrast these two statements: "There are acres of diamonds beneath your feet" versus "Everything you want is right here." Metaphors transport the listener to a different dimension. They grab hold of the mind and stimulate the imagination. The brain thinks in pictures, not words. Use words to create pictures and your speech will be memorable.
- **Use action words**. To persuade people to do something, and to create energy and a sense of movement, use action words. Words and phrases like "let's do it right now," "take charge," and "get going" strengthen your message. Let your listeners visualize the action.
- **Use short, simple words**. You'll sacrifice success if you speak to impress. Avoid the William F. Buckley syndrome. A lot of big, multi-syllabic words will alienate your audience. Why use

a big word when a short one will do?

- **Use words that sell**. According to direct marketers, certain words move people to action and strike an emotional chord. Those words are *you, new, love, save, gain, guarantee, money, results, improved,* and *free.* "You will love the money you save as you gain these new results" is a persuasive sentence.

- **Use strong, definitive words**. Nothing weakens your conviction as quickly as using tentative language. If you use words such as *think, if, sort of, hope, maybe, can't, have to,* and *trying,* your listeners will sense that you lack confidence or commitment. Tentative words sabotage your message and lead listeners to postpone a decision. Substitute stronger words such as *I know* or *I am confident.* Don't say *if*—say *when.* Don't say *have to*—say *I choose to.* Change *can't* to *can.*

- **Ask which words to avoid**. Find out ahead of time about your audience. Ask your contact person about words, expressions, or phrases you should avoid. With diverse audiences, you don't want to risk offending anyone.

- **Incorporate multi-sensory words**. Most audiences learn through one of three channels: visual, auditory, or kinesthetic. A good speaker will incorporate all three modalities into his or her presentation. Use visual words such as *focus, look, imagine,* and *big picture.* Auditory words include *listen, rings a bell, resonate,* and *harmony.* Kinesthetic terms refer to touching and feeling: *massage the data, get your arms around it, gut reaction.* In every speech, let the audience see, hear, and do.

DON'T

- **Plagiarize another person's words**. Not only can you be sued, but it means you don't have anything to say. Find your passion, and your own message will surface. If you quote another person, be sure to give credit.

- **Use ethnic slurs or highly charged words**. In today's multi-cultural world, even the most common expressions may offend some people, for example, "sacred cows" or "lynch mob."

- **Use fillers, hedging, or taglines**. These credibility killers will make you less competent in the eyes of your listeners. Ums and ahs are useless fillers. Pause instead. Words like "think" and "guess" (hedging) and taglines (don't you think?) leave an impression that you're unsure of what you're saying.
- **Slang**. Unless you're making a point, slang will either date you, regionalize you, or mark you as uneducated. Eliminate words like "cop out," "ain't," "ragging on me," "commode," and so on.

3

Fear Fixes: Conquering Nervousness

Feel the fear and do it anyway.
  –Susan Jeffers

What you resist, persists.
  –Diane DiResta

*I*n every seminar I deliver, nine out of ten people are there because they don't want to feel nervous when they give a presentation or speech. They come to my classes in search of the magic elixir to cure their stage fright. Here's the truth: there is no cure.

If I had the cure for stage fright, I wouldn't be sitting at my laptop writing this book. I would be on a tropical island with piña colada in hand, counting my millions. Now before you close this book, let me tell you the good news. You can manage and control your nervousness, and it will decrease over time as you gain public speaking experience.

If you get nervous before a presentation, you're in good company. Let's start with Sir Laurence Olivier. He was so nervous that he would retch before a performance. Barbra Streisand didn't perform on stage for years because of intense stage fright. She would tape the lyrics of her songs to the floor because she was afraid she'd forget the words. Carly Simon dreaded going on stage and had to push herself to perform live.

Elvis Presley once said that he wouldn't want to follow singer Roy Orbison on stage. While Roy Orbison was a respected performer, did Elvis have anything to fear? I think not.

Why would it be any different for you? How is it that these great stars, who were so loved by the public, experienced performance anxiety? Clearly they could have recited the pledge of allegiance and people would still have lined up to see them.

Let's begin by examining what's going on in your mind and body before you have to make a presentation. How high is your PPQ—your Presentation Panic Quotient? To answer that question, take the PPQ quiz.

What's Your Presentation Panic Quotient?

Check one response in each column. Give yourself a 1 for every yes and a 0 for every no.

1. I get butterflies just thinking about presenting.	yes_____	no_____
2. I can't sleep the night before a presentation.	yes_____	no_____
3. I often try to get out of speaking.	yes_____	no_____
4. I experience visceral reactions (sweaty palms, pounding heart, red face).	yes_____	no_____
5. My breathing becomes rapid.	yes_____	no_____
6. I freeze or lose my train of thought.	yes_____	no_____

7. The words don't come out right.	yes_____	no_____
8. I start speaking fast.	yes_____	no_____
9. My mouth gets dry.	yes_____	no_____
10. I feel faint.	yes_____	no_____
11. I feel as if I'm making a fool of myself.	yes_____	no_____
12. I often lose my place in my notes.	yes_____	no_____
13. My voice quivers.	yes_____	no_____
14. It feels like everyone is staring at me.	yes_____	no_____
15. I often feel unprepared.	yes_____	no_____
16. I tell myself I'm nervous.	yes_____	no_____
17. I let others know I'm nervous.	yes_____	no_____
18. I don't remember what I just said.	yes_____	no_____
19. I think the audience knows I'm nervous.	yes_____	no_____
20. I'd rather die than give a speech.	yes_____	no_____

Give yourself one point for every yes you marked. Total the number of points and read the appropriate description below.

Confident (0-5 points): You are in control. You may feel slightly nervous at the beginning, but you're confident that you have the skills to present effectively.

Butterflies (6-11 points): You get nervous most of the time but can plow through and make your point. Your confidence will increase with continued practice and training.

Panic (12-20 points): your nervousness is getting in the way. You try to avoid public speaking whenever possible. Face your fear. Sign up for a public speaking class and work with a supportive coach. You can reduce your nervousness significantly if you keep working at it.

Phobic: Occasionally, panic turns into a true phobia. This is rare. You checked statement 20 yes. Speaking for you is akin to death. You may be too afraid to take a class. Or you may have been trained but it isn't helping. When you are truly traumatized by speaking, seek a psychologist who will use desensitization training to help you overcome your phobia.

Case Study

> ## Phobia
>
> Susan was a successful salesperson. She was very good with her clients, who liked and respected her. She could overcome people's objections and stand her ground when necessary. Her typical sale was with individuals across a desk.
>
> In one-to-one conversations, Susan was fine. When it came to presenting, however, Susan would freeze. She did not express herself well. She stumbled and got very red in the face.
>
> Susan was very concerned about the redness and her fear. During one visualization exercise, she could not imagine an audience of smiling faces. Instead, she saw only angry faces. There was no one in the room but the two of us at the time. This led to emotional turmoil for Susan and her face turned red. Susan was having a phobic reaction.
>
> We eventually brought in a specialist who worked with phobias. Susan traced the origin of her phobia to being humiliated in elementary school by a teacher. Over time and with practice, she overcame her phobia,

Nerves, Not Phobia

When it comes to presenting, most people are not phobic. They're simply nervous. And this nervousness can change over time or with the situation. For example, I usually rate myself a 1 or 2 on the PPQ. However, if I were to speak to 1,600 members of the National Speakers Association, my score would shoot up to at least a 10 or 12.

The first step in controlling your nervousness is to embrace it. That's right. Anything that you resist will have power over you. Nervousness is not your enemy. You need some of that adrenaline rush to keep you dynamic. Make nervousness your friend.

What if you felt no nervousness at all? Your delivery would probably be flat. Why? Because nervousness is energy. When it's intense it becomes negative energy because we have turned it against ourselves. But you can take a negative and make it a positive. In the case of public speaking, you can channel your nervous energy outward by being dynamic.

So step one in conquering your nervousness is accepting that you feel nervous. It's OK. Step two is taking comfort in knowing that you're in good company. Everyone feels nervous at some time or another when making a presentation. And I mean *everyone*. Step three is managing your nervous energy. Let's talk about some specific strategies for doing that.

Mental, Physical, Behavioral, and Chemical Remedies for Nervousness

Managing your nervous energy will help you manage the fear you have about making speeches or presentations. Fear fixes fall into three major categories: **mental**, **physical**, and **behavioral**. There are several **chemical** remedies as well. You can control your nervousness by using one or several of the following techniques.

Mental	Physical	Behavioral	Chemical
visualization	breathing	rehearsal	diet
meditation	yoga	interaction	Rescue Remedy
affirmations	exercise	passion	Valerian Root
self-crediting	work the room	acting lessons	
love the audience	eye contact	meet the audience first	
phobia fix	gesturing	visual aids	
soothing music	pausing	partnering	
	smiling	support group	
	yawning	emulate top speakers	
	setting an anchor	do your homework	

Mental Remedies

We start here because nervousness begins in your mind, with a negative mental picture. It then translates into physical reactions, such as rapid breathing, which can then cause you to change your behavior—for example, you might avoid public speaking. You can also undergo biochemical changes, such as getting acid stomach.

There are two categories of nervousness. People go into either hyperdrive (flailing arms, rapid speech) or deep freeze (monotone, locked arms, little animation). If you experience either of these types of nervousness, use the exercises described here.

Now let's take a closer look at the mental strategies you can use to manage and conquer your nervousness about making speeches and presentations.

Visualization. This is the process of running a movie through your mind. You are the producer, director, and actor. You determine the outcome. Most people use the technique of visualization without realizing it. But they're usually envisioning a negative image of themselves or the audience. You can change that! How? Try the following technique:

1. Find a quiet place and mentally rehearse your presentation.
2. See yourself as you rise from your seat and approach the audience.
3. See how poised you look.
4. Experience the feeling of confidence as you breathe and greet the audience. Hear your opening words as they smoothly fall from your lips.
5. Breathe again as you hear yourself transition to the body and then to the summary of your talk.
6. See all the smiling faces nodding with approval.
7. Hear the laughter as you make a humorous point.
8. Hear the thunderous applause as you finish your speech.
9. Feel the positive energy coming toward you from the audience.
10. Breathe again and smile as you feel the positive emotions that come from a job well done.

11. Watch yourself as you walk confidently to your chair.
12. Congratulate yourself.

I know some of you are scoffing. You're thinking, "What is this new age mumbo-jumbo?"

But visualization is a powerful technique. Sports psychologists use this process all the time. In one research study, two teams were examined. One team practiced regularly, shooting baskets. The other team spent its time mentally practicing. Members of this team envisioned sinking the ball in the hoop. They did not engage in physical practice. At the end of the study, the team that mentally visualized success scored as well as the team that practiced physically. That's the power of the mind! This doesn't mean you don't have to practice. It means that your practice will be more focused and fruitful when combined with visualization. Here's the formula:

Visualization + Skill + Practice = Success

If you have a problem with positive visualization, try the reverse. Imagine people in their underwear. It's a great equalizer and reminds us that we're all human. Don't give the audience so

Case Study

Jim Carrey

Jim Carrey, the famous comedian turned actor, became one of the highest paid comedic film actors through visualization. He tells a story about how he would drive to the Hollywood Hills at night and park his car. He would imagine in his mind receiving a $10 million check for doing a film. He would visualize receiving his accolades and how it would feel to receive that check.

Carrey would act out the entire scenario in his mind. He even wrote a check to himself for the sum of $10 million and kept it in his wallet! He went through this visualization often as he worked hard to achieve his goal.

The result? He was eventually paid $10 million for starring in the motion picture, *The Mask*. He then received $20 million for *The Cable Guy*.

much power. (Note: Be careful with this technique. One participant told me he tried it and he started laughing out loud. But at
least he relaxed!)

Some of you probably think, "Visualization can work for others, but I can't visualize." If you're one of these people, try the following exercise:

Exercise

> Imagine you are traveling down a road. You come to a light. (Close
> your eyes and see the light.)
> What color is the light? _____
>
> You drive past a rose garden. You get out of the car to smell the
> roses. (Close your eyes and see the roses.)
> What color are the roses? _____
>
> As you walk past a stream there is a child up ahead. (Close your eyes
> and see the child.)
> How old is the child? _____

That was a visualization. You created your own picture. You
have the power to change the pictures in your mind. Take that
picture of nervousness and replace it with one of confidence.

In the movie *South Pacific*, Mitzi Gaynor sings, "I'm gonna
wash that man right out of my hair" as a metaphor for ending a
relationship. She does something physical and mental (washing
the man out of her hair) to eliminate him from her life. You can do

Exercise

> Write out your own visualization. Be sure to include three compo-
> nents: what you see, hear, and feel. Practice this visualization before
> your presentation and watch what happens.
>
> _____
>
> _____
>
> _____

the same thing with fear and nervousness. Create a metaphor for yourself. Maybe you'll bury your fear in the ground or throw it into the trash can. Think it! Do it!

Meditation. While visualization is the conscious creation of positive pictures, meditation is the clearing of your mind. This is a mental process that yields many physical benefits. By emptying your mind, you relax and center your body. Meditation can slow your heartbeat, speech tempo, and body movements. It can also still your "mental chatter." (Mental chatter is the random thoughts that occur in our minds when we're trying to relax.)

Imagine a white screen in front of you. Focus on that screen or focus on an object. Clear your mind of any thoughts. When a thought pops up, say, "I am thinking" and return to the screen. Don't fight the thoughts that come into your head. Recognize them and let them go.

Another way to meditate is to focus on your breathing. Take in a deep breath, hold it, and exhale slowly to the count of eight. Do this before your speech to calm your nerves. There are many good meditation audiotapes. (Don't listen to them while you're driving!)

Affirmations. Positive statements, when spoken aloud over time, can change reality. The term "affirm" means to "make firm." You're already using this technique by giving yourself "nervous" messages.

GIGO is a term used in technology. It stands for "Garbage In, Garbage Out." The brain is like a big computer. If you program your brain with negative thoughts, it will accept them as truth. The unconscious mind cannot distinguish fantasy from reality.

So start saying positive affirmations about yourself. Replace criticizing with crediting.

A positive affirmation can be a sentence, a phrase, or a word. One speaker uses the word *kryptonite* as her affirmation. It is the only substance strong enough to kill Superman. The word makes

Case Study

Turn Nervousness into Energy

When I joined the National Speakers Association, I was eager to get involved. I volunteered to do a 10-minute showcase in front of 70 people. They would listen to my material and would then fill out evaluation sheets.

I was a wreck. These were professional speakers and were accustomed to hearing good presenters. I told my friend, "I'm so nervous. My stomach's in knots. Why did I volunteer to do this?" She took hold of my shoulders and said, "Diane, don't do that to yourself. You are not nervous. You are energized!"

I realized she was right. If I kept focusing on my nervousness, I wouldn't be giving it my best shot. So I took in a deep breath and kept saying to myself, "I'm energized. I'm energized."

The next morning, I felt some initial anxiety. That positive affirmation enabled me to channel my nerves into dynamic energy. The result? My evaluations were the highest of the three presenters that day.

---

her feel powerful.

Some good affirmations for overcoming nervousness include: *I'm energized, I can do this, I know my material, Just do it, Kick butt.* (**Caution:** Don't formulate a statement in the negative. I'm not nervous is a negative affirmation. The brain will hear the word nervous and will accept that as truth. Change your affirmation to the positive, I am confident.)

Self-crediting. This is a form of affirmation. Right after your presentation, credit yourself for something you did well. We're often too willing to beat up on ourselves. Criticism contracts, praise expands. Even if your knees were shaking and you stuttered, credit yourself for something that went well.

Negative: "I blew that. I was awful. They knew I was nervous. I'll never be good at this. I looked like a fool up there."

Self-crediting: "It was my first time. I got through it. I finished

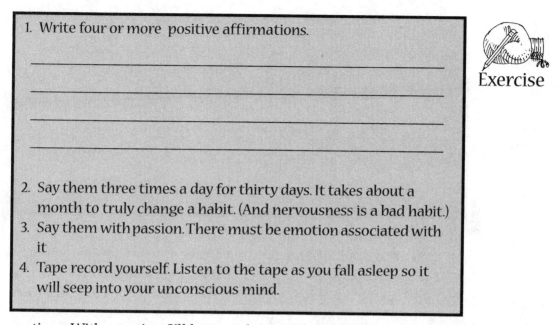

1. Write four or more positive affirmations.

_____

_____

_____

_____

2. Say them three times a day for thirty days. It takes about a month to truly change a habit. (And nervousness is a bad habit.)
3. Say them with passion. There must be emotion associated with it
4. Tape record yourself. Listen to the tape as you fall asleep so it will seep into your unconscious mind.

Exercise

on time. With practice, I'll become better. I know what to do next time."

It does nothing for your confidence to criticize and berate yourself. What you focus your attention on grows. It's a matter of self-fulfilling prophecy. Negative expectations produce negative performance. Negative performance results in negative self-talk. Only you can break the cycle.

Loving the audience. Although this is listed as a mental technique, it's really about feeling. The audience is not out to get you. They want you to succeed. Even if it's a hostile audience, love and caring will turn them around.

Nervousness is self-centered. When you're nervous, you are focusing on yourself. You're worried about how you look, how you sound, being the center of attention. Stop it! Think about those people who came to hear your message. Change your focus to how you can serve them. What do they need?

What will make your presentation more enjoyable for them or helpful to them? Send loving thoughts. One performer would

Exercise

Think about your last presentation. Credit yourself right now for what you did well. Write out a couple of statements to describe what you did well and say them out loud (no self-flagellation allowed).

_____

_____

_____

envision white light around the audience before she walked out on stage. You don't believe people can sense what you're feeling?

Have you ever been on a bus or train and suddenly looked over at someone only to find the person looking back at you? You could feel the person's eyes on you even though he or she never spoke.

We're sending out energy all the time. People intuitively pick up on fear. It goes back to our reptilian brain. First the eyes scan for threat. People can also feel warmth and sincerity. Make them your friends. Mentally broadcast your intent. ("I'm glad to be here. I like you. I am here to serve.") The audience will receive your message before you ever begin speaking.

Phobia fix. In extreme cases of nervousness—that is, if you have a phobia—you'll need the special skills of a psychologist or an neurolinguistic programming (NLP) expert. Techniques such as a phobia fix or a trauma fix can often yield dramatic results.

The process can take several sessions. It involves having the person dissociate himself or herself from the fear-inducing event and think of it in a new, more positive way. To find an NLP practitioner in your area, turn to "Appendix of Resources" at the end of this book.

Soothing music. Research demonstrates that certain pieces of

Exercise

> Write a positive, loving message that you can silently send out to the audience. You can't fake it . It must come from your heart.
>
> _____
>
> _____
>
> _____

classical music can help you relax. Some of the baroque and classical compositions have tempos of 60 to 70 beats per minute, a rhythm that mimics the human heart rate.

Pachelbel's *Canon in D Major*, Vivaldi's *Four Seasons*, Bach's *Organ Works*, *Fantasy in G*, and Handel's *Concerti Op. 4* are good selections for relaxing your mind. If possible, listen to soothing music the night before your presentation and right before the presentation itself.

Physical Remedies

Anxiety is accompanied by an interruption in respiration.
–Roger Wolger, Ph.D.

Breathing. Think about the last time you experienced fear. What did you do? You held your breath. When nerves set in, we go into a fright, fight, or flight state. We tense up, the adrenaline increases, and we get ready to either fight or flee. This primitive survival reaction does not serve you well as a speaker.

Holding you breath will result in vocal quivering, shortness of breath, and rapid speech. Most of us have forgotten how to breathe properly. Shallow breathing won't sustain you as a presenter. Shallow breathing is defined by shoulder and chest movement. If your shoulders and chest rise as you breathe, you are a shallow breather.

Power breathing comes from the diaphragm or the lower

abdominal muscles. Barbra Streisand can hold a long note because she's breathing from the diaphragm. You can speak only on exhalation, not on inhalation. Try speaking as you inhale. Impossible. In order to speak properly, you need to have enough air to exhale.

To get a feel for proper breathing, lie down on a flat surface. Now put a book on your abdomen and breathe naturally. You'll see the book rise and fall. The abdomen is where you want to concentrate your breathing. We all breathe correctly when lying down.

Yoga. Yoga is more than a physical exercise. It combines the physical and mental systems. It's great for stretching and loosening the muscles as well as focusing your mind and breathing. You can

Exercise

1. Sit up straight in a chair.
2. Put both feet flat on the floor.
3. Place one hand on your abdomen and one hand on your chest.
4. Loosen tight buckles or waistbands.
5. Close your eyes or focus on a spot.
6. Take in air.
7. As you inhale the lower hand should move out.
8. As you exhale the lower hand should recede.
9. Do this for the count of 10. One...breathe in and breathe out. Two....breathe in and breathe out.

Where did you notice the most movement? Was it concentrated in the lower region? If your shoulders moved upward, have a partner hold your shoulders down and do the exercise again. Practice daily. When you learn how to breathe correctly, you will have more power as a presenter. You will also be able to center your body and relax your nerves.

Variation: Clasp your hands together and put them on your abdomen. Slow your breathing to the count of ten. You can do this in your seat before you get up to speak. Nobody will know that you're doing breathing exercises.

Another way to relax your mind and body is to do the "4-7-8" exercise. While sitting or standing, breathe in through your nose to the count of four—1, 2, 3, 4. Hold the breath for the count of seven. Finally, exhale from your mouth to the count of eight.

Continue to repeat the 4-7-8 exercise at least five times or as needed. You might feel a little lightheaded the first time you try it. But you'll definitely feel relaxed and you'll slow down your breathing. This is an exercise used in yoga classes. It has the effect of a short meditation.

Exercise

achieve deep states of relaxation when you apply the techniques. Most colleges and health clubs offer classes in yoga.

Exercise. One of the quickest ways to burn off nervous energy is to get physical. One speaker used to walk the corridors while the previous presenter was speaking. Nervous energy needs an outlet. The walking was an energizer. One motivational speaker would jog before his presentations. He needed to pump up his body to pump up the crowd.

While you probably aren't going to run a marathon before giving a speech, you can do some light exercise. Here are some you might try:

- *Standing push-ups*. Extend your arms and push off against a wall. Do this several times.
- *Standing sit-ups*. Sit in a chair, then stand up and sit down repetitively. Do this ten times and then rest. Try doing three repetitions of ten.
- *Rag doll exercise*. Drop from the waist like a rag doll. Let your arms and head hang. Bend slightly at the knees. Make a hissing sound as you let all the air escape. Now come up slowly one vertebra at a time until you're upright again.
- *Progressive relaxation*. You can do this either standing or sitting. Start with your ankles. Tense them. Now tense your calves. Tighten your thighs, hips, abdomen, stomach, chest, and

shoulders. Squeeze your fists and tighten your arms, neck, and face. Hold the tension. Now let go. You will immediately feel a surge of relaxed energy as you let go.

- *Head rolls.* Drop your chin to your chest. Without lifting your head, roll to the right shoulder, then to your back, then roll to the right and forward. Now reverse the position. Feel the tension released from your neck.
- *Shoulder lifts.* Lift your shoulders up and back and down and forward in a continuous rolling motion. Do this 8-10 times. Then reverse the movement.

Work the room. This involves moving during your speech. Begin your talk from the front of the room. Once you get started and feel a need to move, go with it. But don't pace! Focus your movement. You must have a reason for the movement—and nervousness doesn't count.

As you make a point, walk in closer to the audience. Choose a person to move toward. Stop and continue to make your point. As you segue to the next topic, walk over to another side of the room. This signals that you're making a new point.

You can walk into the crowd and ask a question. Look out at the audience and wait for a reply. You can then walk back to the podium to look at your notes and to create distance.

The most dynamic speakers work the room. This technique goes beyond channeling your nervous energy. It also creates interest. It stimulates people to listen because you're doing something different. You have interrupted the normal pattern. It also makes you look confident. (I know you may not feel that way, but the audience won't be able to tell.) Finally, it creates an intimacy with the audience. They will feel more of a connection with you.

Eye contact. In Chapter 2, we discussed how you could use eye contact effectively. You can reduce your nervousness by singling out individuals. Look for friendly faces and avoid the bored or skeptical people. Have a conversation with the key individuals in the crowd.

Stay with each person for a sentence or two and then move on. Most of us aren't nervous talking to one person. You don't have to stare at the person eye to eye. You can look at their nose or at the center of their forehead. They won't know the difference. Ask people you know to sit up front so that you can find them easily. Begin with them. Knowing people are on your side will boost your confidence.

Gesturing. How can gesturing lower your anxiety? It's the same principle as working the room. Energy wants to be released. Practice freeing up your hands. Go back to Chapter 2 and use the exercises.

It also helps to have a "rest position." This is a position you can go back into when you're not gesturing or if you start to fidget. For example, place your hands together waist high. Another rest position may be putting one hand in a pocket. The next time you start flailing or fidgeting, go right into your rest position. Once you begin to gesture, forget about your hands and get involved with the audience and the message. Concentrate on having a conversation and your gestures will happen naturally.

Pausing. Are you in a nervous race to the finish line? Slow down, and then slow down again. Pausing reduces your nervousness by giving you breathing and thinking time. Take in a breath. Let the audience process your last point.

Pausing is most critical at the end of a sentence. Many speakers are not really too fast. They just don't stop. They speak one long run-on sentence. It's like reading a book without punctuation marks. It makes comprehension difficult.

In Chapter 2, we discussed holding a pause for four beats. At first, that pause will seem like an eternity. That's why you need to videotape yourself. If you do, you'll see that the pause is not as long as it feels. You'll also notice how much more confident you appear when you slow down and pause. Speed demons look and sound nervous.

Smiling. You don't have to grin like a Cheshire cat, but smiling does make you look confident. It has a warming effect on the audience. The face of fear is frozen and serious. This can be intimidating to the audience. So think about making people feel comfortable with you. Smile when you introduce yourself. Smile when someone asks you a question. Of course, you don't want to be smiling if you're there to announce layoffs. But in most cases, a smile has a long-reaching effect on the audience and on you as well.

Tony Robbins, author of the book *Unlimited Power*, talks about physiological and mental states. By changing your physical state, he says, you can change how you feel. It's difficult to feel confident if you stoop, drop your shoulders, look down, and lower your voice. So smile! Smiling will not eradicate nervousness, but it will send a positive message to your brain. And that, over time, will help you relax.

Yawning. It's difficult to yawn and be tense at the same time. Yawning and laughing relieve tension. Yawn right before you are called on to speak. (Be sure to finish yawning before you arrive on the platform and make sure no one in the audience sees you.) By yawning, you're changing your physiology and getting into a more relaxed state.

Setting an anchor. We're all anchored to different stimuli. Recall an old song on the radio and you are instantly flooded with fond memories. You pass by a woman wearing Chanel No. 5 perfume and you instantly think of your college sweetheart. When I see chartreuse I think about my fifth-grade swimsuit.

A smell, a sound, a taste, a picture, a touch, even a color can be an anchor. Right now you're anchored to fear. You can create your own positive anchor. The simplest way to do that is to transfer your nervous energy somewhere specific. For example, you can squeeze your thumb and index finger together when you get tense. No one will realize you're doing it and it gives the nervousness someplace to go. It's a more positive anchor than fidgeting.

How to Set an Anchor

1. Recall a pleasant experience. It doesn't have to be a speaking experience.
2. Notice what you see, hear, or feel as you recall that experience.
3. Plan where you will anchor the experience. You may touch your wrist with your finger. You may squeeze your thumb and index finger together. (Note: You must be able to do whatever you choose easily and repeatedly, so don't chose a yoga contortion. Keep it simple.)
4. Recall the same pleasant experience again. As soon as the feelings come up, set the anchor. (See Step 3.)
5. Now test the anchor. Touch your wrist or the place you selected for the anchor. The pleasant feeling should now surface without recalling the entire pleasant experience. (If it doesn't work, it means you set the anchor too soon or too late. You must set the anchor the moment you feel the emotions of that pleasant event. Go back to Step 1.)
6. Set the anchor right before you get up to speak. You should be able to "touch and go."

Behavioral Remedies

Rehearsal. This sounds like common sense—and it is. There's no substitute for practice. The thing that will most increase your anxiety is lack of preparation.

One speaker I worked with had not planned to rehearse her presentation. She had researched it and written it out, and she knew her subject matter. I insisted, however, that she rehearse the presentation out loud. Otherwise, how would she know if it flowed? How would she know if the timing was good?

Rehearse out loud by speaking into a tape recorder or standing in front of a mirror. Most important, time yourself. Once you're confident in your material and your timing is right, put away your notes. Don't over-rehearse.

Vanna White, star of _Wheel of Fortune_, agrees that there's no substitute for practice. She says, "I overcame stage fright from speaking and answering questions from our studio audience of 300 people. It takes experience. No one ever feels comfortable the first time. Each time gets easier."

Interaction. You don't have to stay glued to the podium reading your script. Come out to the audience and engage them. Ask a question and wait for a response. Ask another question. Use humor. Be present in the moment and spontaneous. React to what's happening in the audience.

Joke with people. Build in a quick, interactive exercise. For example, if your topic is time management, ask a few volunteers to do a sentence completion activity:

_If only I had more time, I would _ _____.

This kind of activity gets your audience involved and gives you insight into what they value. It's an attention-getting way to introduce the need for your topic.

At certain times, you may want to ask people true-or-false questions. Give each audience member two index cards of different colors—blue and yellow, for example. Tell people to raise the blue card for true statements and the yellow card for false statements. Now you have audience participation.

Interaction is fun and easy. Audience members will enjoy it and you'll feel less nervous because people are sharing the presentation with you. Doesn't it feel good to take the pressure off?

Passion. The best speakers aren't the most polished or eloquent orators. Nor are they the most intelligent or educated. But they all share one characteristic: passion. The qualities that move people to take action or to buy from you are conviction and passion.

It was passion that created MADD–Mothers Against Drunk Driving. It was one woman who changed the law and made driving drunk a more severe crime punishable by imprisonment and long-term loss of license. Her daughter was killed by a drunk driver.

Case Study

> ### Enthusiasm
>
> Judy was a salesperson for a training company. She sold to large corporations that wanted to improve the management skills of their people. One time, Judy was up against quite a few vendors. Unfortunately, her company was the most expensive. Still, she continued to explain what the company offered and why it was the best vendor. Judy made the sale.
>
> After the contract was signed, Judy took the buyer aside and said, "I'm curious. Why did you buy from us when we were the highest bidder?" The buyer responded, "Because you were so enthusiastic!"

John Walsh, host of television's *America's Most Wanted*, had no experience in television. But his passionate drive to avenge the murder of his son, Adam, is what changed the 24-hour waiting period to report missing children. Police departments now can search for a missing child immediately.

Neither of these people was a professional speaker. But both moved mountains because of their passion. What do you feel passionate about? Where you have passion, you have power. Passion is a great elixir. When you get excited about your message, you lose yourself.

When Dolly Parton was asked if she felt fear trying to pursue her dream of a singing career, she said, "Yes, but my desire to achieve my dream was stronger than the fear." When you have passion, your enthusiasm comes through. You become more expressive and dynamic.

You don't feel passion? Then find another topic. If you've been assigned a topic, build passion by creating examples or sharing stories that excite you.

Acting lessons. Developing stage presence builds your confidence. Acting lessons will show you how to move your body, project your voice, be spontaneous, and command an audience.

Exercise

Think of something that pushes your buttons. Something you feel strongly about. Maybe it is poor customer service. Or traffic jams. Or poverty. Maybe it's your in-laws or forgetting to put the cap on the toothpaste.

Write down the topic you feel passionate about on the line below.

Topic: _____

Talk for one to two minutes about how strongly you feel about this issue. Get into the emotion. Let it rip.

Videotape yourself. If you are self-conscious about talking to yourself, do this with a friend. Now watch your videotape. Amazing, isn't it? Did you notice all that expression coming out?

Didn't you look more confident? You weren't thinking about what to do with your hands. Was your friend convinced? Now write down what you liked about your presentation. (Remember to self-credit.)

_____

_____

_____

Light a fire under yourself and the audience will ignite.

Many people are afraid of public speaking because of ignorance. They simply don't know the skills. By practicing the skills of stage mechanics, you'll know that you can handle yourself on the platform.

Acting classes are available at most local colleges or acting schools. Some schools will even allow you to audit a class.

Meet the audience first. Fear of public speaking is often fear of the unknown. Who will be in the audience? Will they be *for* me or *against* me? Will I look like a fool?

Since you probably have these and/or similar questions, why

not meet the audience before the speech? Find out who's attending and call them up. If you're presenting to a large audience, talk to a random sampling of audience members. Ask them what they would like to hear. This accomplishes two things: it gives you valuable information on how to slant your speech, and it introduces you as the speaker and initiates a relationship.

Once you've talked to people, you can implement stage two of your getting-to-know-the-audience plan: arrive early for your speech. Greet the people who helped you. You can then mention their names and thank them in your speech. Mingle with the other people in the room as well. Isn't easier to talk to people you know instead of strangers?

Visual aids. Visual aids can really take the edge off your nervousness because they can serve as your notes. By having those bullet points on your slides or charts, you'll always know where you are in your presentation.

Visual aids also give you something to do with your hands as you gesture to a chart. They provide another focus besides yourself. It's easier to present when you have the support of visuals. When used well, they can enhance any presentation. Read Chapter 8 to learn how to use visual aids effectively.

Partnering. Teaming up with a partner can cut your nervousness in half. Who says you have to do your presentation alone? When appropriate, request a partner. If you have to give a monthly progress report, you can give the overview and your partner can give the current recommendations. Then you can come back and summarize.

A variation of this approach is to ask an expert in the audience to share his or her views, insights, and impressions. (Just be sure to get the person's agreement beforehand. Never spring this approach as a surprise. The person may feel put on the spot—especially if he or she isn't prepared.) Once you come to the appropriate part in your presentation, say, "I thought that since we're fortunate to have an expert on benchmarking in the audience, we could ask Roberta to speak to us for ten minutes." Roberta can then speak at the podium or from her seat if it's a small group.

If your assistants worked with you on a project, you can give a short team presentation. Divide it into segments and give each person a chance to speak. This takes the pressure off you and gives recognition and visibility to the other team members.

Support group. One of the best support groups for public speaking is Toastmasters, an international association devoted to enhancing the skills of public speakers from all walks of life. Meetings are held bimonthly and are open to guests. At each session, there are volunteer speakers who receive supportive group feedback. It is this continued practice with people you know that really increases your confidence. Some members become proficient enough to compete in contests. For information on your local Toastmasters chapter, see "Appendix of Resources" in the back of this book.

Emulate top speakers. Another good way to reduce your nervousness about presenting is to spend time in the company of great speakers. Watch the best speakers in your organization. Analyze what they're doing and why they come across so well. Is it the way they tell a story? Is it their humor or organization? Watch political debates on television. Listen to tapes and videos of top speakers. You can find them in bookstores or through educational materials catalogs.

Notice the techniques the speakers use. What can you take from them and adapt to your own style? You'll learn more from watching other speakers than from any other source.

If you wanted to be a champion skier, you wouldn't ski with your peers. You'd take the lift with the best. You can take strokes off your golf game by going out on the course with a master golfer. It's the same with speaking. Surround yourself with the masters and you'll start to master public speaking.

Do your homework. You'll greatly reduce your anxiety if you prepare in advance. Don't wait until the last minute to research your topic—it's too nerve-racking. Instead, find information well beforehand and study it immediately. Talk to the right people. Know your audience and tailor each presentation for that group. Decide what points are most important to make and learn how much time you'll have to make them in your speech.

Chemical Remedies

Note: Check with a physician or nutritionist before taking any herbal or chemical substances.

Diet. Foods can affect your nervous system. A cup of chamomile tea has a soothing effect. It's best to eat lightly before a presentation. Soup, salads, and sandwiches work well. Avoid heavy pasta and steak dishes. They take more energy to digest and will make you tired.

If you're going to be speaking all day and you need to preserve your energy, try having oatmeal for breakfast. Oatmeal stabilizes the blood sugar and will keep you on an even keel. Pastries and other high-sugar foods will initially elevate your blood sugar level, but you will quickly experience an energy crash. They are best eaten in the late afternoon, when you need a quick burst of energy.

There are three foods you'll want to avoid before making your presentation: coffee, milk products, and alcohol. Coffee contains caffeine and will make you jittery. Milk products cause mucus and will force you to have to clear your throat often. And alcohol is a depressant. Although it will make you feel better, it's a false security. Keep the cork in the champagne until after your speech.

Rescue Remedy. There's a tincture produced by Bach Flower Essences that you can find in health food stores. Put four drops in half a glass of water and sip it at intervals as needed. Or, place a couple of drops on your tongue. It will relax you.

Valerian Root. You can take this herb in tea or in a capsule. It has a tranquilizing effect without the side effects of drugs. Most health food stores carry it.

Special Situations

My palms get very sweaty when I have to speak. Nobody will notice if your hands are moist when you're presenting. But if you're speaking at a meeting and you have to shake hands, this can be a problem. There are several things you can do.

You could try rubbing your hands with corn starch, which will absorb the moisture. You can keep a small box in your desk. But carrying corn starch isn't always practical (especially if you're wearing navy blue), so there is another option: liquid talc. Rub a few drops of the lotion in the palms of your hands and it dries instantly like powder. Liquid talc is sold in bath and body shops. Finally, you can purchase a small rosin bag that bowlers use. Rub it between your hands to absorb perspiration.

My hands get very cold. This makes sense, physiologically speaking. When you're nervous or feeling threatened, your body responds by releasing adrenaline, increasing your heartbeat, and directing blood flow to your vital organs and away from your extremities. If your hands are cold, run them under hot water to warm them and rub them together. Wearing gloves also helps retain some of the heat. (Just be sure to take them off before your speech!)

I get so nervous, I turn beet red. The easiest solution to this problem is to wear a scarf or high collar on the day of your presentation. Doing so takes care of a ruddy neck. If your face turns red, try looking up. When we're into our emotions, we tend to look down. When we're searching for a thought, we tend to look up.

By looking up, you access your intellect. At the same time, you take yourself out of the emotions causing the flushing.

I suffer from cotton mouth. As soon as I get up to speak, my mouth goes dry. Two days before your presentation, hydrate your body by taking in lots of water. Then, before you present, request a glass of water on the podium or dais. Top speakers sip water during their presentations. Sipping water creates anticipation as the audience waits for your next thought. It also causes you to pause.

Drink room-temperature water with a bit of lemon. Ice water causes your throat muscles to constrict. You can also lubricate your throat by sucking on a lozenge before the presentation. If that doesn't work, bite down gently on both sides of your tongue. This biting motion causes instant salivation. A mental variation of this technique is to imagine eating a lemon.

I'm clumsy when I'm nervous. What if I drop something? You may drop your notes or a prop due to nervousness. If that happens, pick it up slowly.

I remember attending my first Broadway show. In the middle of a dialogue, the actress lost her pearl necklace. It fell to the floor. Instead of panicking, she kept saying her lines, gently picked up the necklace, and fastened it around her neck. Without missing a beat, she continued her dialogue. I was so impressed! Fast, jerky movements create a perception of nervousness. Slower, more fluid movements indicate confidence.

Accidents will happen. The way you respond to them is what makes you a pro.

Nervous Speaker's First Aid Kit
- Corn starch or rosin bag,
- Bottled water (to hydrate your throat),
- Lozenges (slippery elm or horehound are good for sore throats),

- B vitamins (to reduce stress),
- Soothing herbal tea such as chamomile (not too hot), and
- a portable tape/CD player with meditation music.

It's natural to feel nervous when you are going to make a presentation. The problem is that most people don't realize this and believe the feeling is unique to them. If you recognize that nervousness is natural, you can use it as a source of energy, and at the same time take actions to reduce the fears you may also be experiencing. The following checklist summarizes the suggestions I've covered in this chapter.

Checklist for Managing Nervousness

DO

- **Breathe deeply**. Place one hand on your diaphragm and breathe slowly to the count of ten. This will relax your mind and slow you down. You need to breathe from the diaphragm to get enough breath support. This is your power generator.
- **Visualize**. Imagine every aspect of your presentation. See yourself as you walk to the lectern. Watch as you deliver your talk to the audience. Hear the applause as you finish the speech. Feel the sense of accomplishment and satisfaction as you confidently end the speech. Do this several times a week. Visual imagery is a powerful technique that is used often by professional athletes.
- **Rehearse, rehearse, rehearse.** There's no substitute for preparation. The better you know your subject, the more confident you'll be. Rehearse out loud in front of a mirror. Better yet, rehearse on videotape or audiotape.
- **Arrive early.** Prepare and set up ahead of schedule. Get the feel of the lectern and test the microphone. Walk around. Greet participants individually. Get to know them and they will be on your side.

- **Involve the audience**. Ask a question or take a quick poll. This will take the focus off you for a moment and help you gain rapport with the group.
- **Use visual aids.** Visuals make your presentation more interesting and also serve as notes. Interact with the visuals to burn off some of your nervous energy. Point, gesture, and move into the visuals.
- **Smile.** You'll look better and feel better when you smile. A smile warms up the audience and makes them feel comfortable with you.
- **Speak often.** Confidence increases with practice. Volunteer to speak at every opportunity. Join your local Toastmasters group. You can't become an excellent presenter just by reading a book. So go out and do it.
- **Give yourself credit.** You know more about your subject than the audience does. If you forget a point, they'll never know it. They're coming to hear you because you have something to offer them.
- **Find a friendly face.** Talk directly to the person who smiled at you. Then find another person who seems receptive. Concentrate on using balanced eye contact and you'll soon forget yourself.
- **Affirm yourself**. Monitor your internal messages. Tell yourself that you're confident, energized, excited. Write a positive affirmation about yourself and say it continuously. ("I'm a confident and capable presenter.")
- **Send loving thoughts to the audience.** Energy can be felt, and thoughts are energy. An audience can sense when you care, and they'll return your loving energy.
- **Focus on others.** Nervousness is a preoccupation with yourself.
- **Imagine people in their underwear.** If all else fails, try this one. It can't hurt—and it may remind you that we're all human. Don't give so much power to the audience.

- **Burn off energy.** You can walk, push against a wall, or move in any way that will make you feel energized but relaxed.

DON'T

- **Announce your nervousness.** People in the audiences will start to look for signs.
- **Think negative thoughts.** You're not nervous; you're energized. Put a rubber band around your wrist. Every time you have a negative thought ("I'm nervous"), snap the rubber band. Replace the negative thought with a positive one. After enough wrist-snapping, you'll change those distorted messages.
- **Be afraid of silence.** If you lose your place, a long pause can add drama. Change what you were going to say. As long as the concept is the same, the audience will never know the difference.

Listening:
The Other Side
of Speaking

Man's inability to communicate is a result of his
failure to listen effectively.
    –Carl Rogers

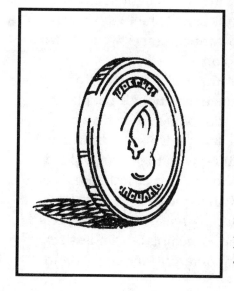

*T*his is a book about public speaking—so why are we about to discuss listening? Isn't listening the audience's job? Of course it is.

But it's your job too.

Speaking is not one-dimensional. If you don't have good listening skills, you won't be an effective speaker. The average person listens at 25 to 50% capacity; people immediately remember 50% of what they hear, and they recall only 25% of it shortly afterward. So you have to help your audience listen.

How? By first taking responsibility for your own listening. Are you listening to the signals from your audience? The audience listens to you and you must listen back. Even if there is no dialogue, you have to be able to "listen" to your audience members' nonverbals. (Remember: nonverbal communication is more than half the message.)

The first time you need to listen is when you're researching your audience. What do your listeners think is important? What kinds of speakers have been successful with them in the past? How do they feel about your topic?

After you prepare your content, you must listen to yourself. Do you sound credible, enthusiastic, and knowledgeable?

You must then listen to your audience. What are they communicating? Rodgers and Hammerstein were masters at hearing nuances in the audience. On opening night, instead of watching the performance they would listen to the audience. During the first performance of *The King and I*, they sensed a restlessness in the audience. They realized that the crowd wanted to feel a sense of romance between Anna and the King. That night, the two returned to their room and created the song "Shall We Dance." The show became a success. This romantic number was just what the audience wanted. Listening paid off.

What is your audience telling you? A lot of coughing or rustling may signal discomfort. Change direction. If people are doodling, side-talking, or avoiding eye contact, they may be bored. Pick up the pace. Change the tempo. Do something different. What if your listeners are all sitting with their arms folded, scowling or glaring at you? Uh-oh. You've just encountered resistance. Find out why. Use humor. Change the energy.

Listening is the greatest gift you can give an audience, because when you listen you give of yourself. Listening is a selfless act. You must suspend your own ego and interests and focus on the other person.

Speakers who are seen as arrogant are often so focused on themselves that they can't or won't listen to anyone else. They think they're the stars and that the audience is waiting for their wise words and humorous jests. In fact, they are deluding themselves.

People can feel energy. They know when you're sincere and when you care about them. There's always an exchange of energy between a speaker and a listener, a performer and an audience. You can't see energy but you can feel the vibrations in the room. You know when it's expanding or moving back and forth. You can also feel it contracting. Listening is the skill that enables you to develop a relationship with the audience.

When you're "listening" for body language, look for patterns, not individual gestures.

For example, folded arms can mean being closed off. But it can also mean that the person feels cold. Instead of assigning a single meaning to body language, look for abrupt movements or changes in behavior. These are clues that tell you to slow down, speed up, or change course.

The Four Steps of Listening

According to the International Listening Association, "Listening is the process of receiving, constructing meaning from, and responding to spoken and nonverbal messages." It doesn't matter if your presentation is a one-to-one meeting, a product demonstration, or a job interview. In order to be effective, you must be an effective listener. If you don't listen to people, you won't connect with them.

Can you find the hidden word in LISTEN? Unscramble the letters, and you'll find the word SILENT. You must be willing to be silent before you can begin to listen. That means silencing your mind chatter as well as your voice.

Being a good listener involves four aspects: attention, comprehension, interpretation, and retention.

Attention. This means being alert, getting ready to listen, and getting focused by listening for a purpose. That purpose may be to gain understanding of the customers' needs or to understand how the audience is feeling. Focus your attention on the listeners by ridding the room of any physical distractions. Sit at a clean table and move aside any coffee cups or papers. Hold your telephone calls. Close the door to prevent intrusions. If you're on a platform, tape down wires and move excess papers or notes to avoid clutter. Remove emotional distractions by mentally concentrating on the task at hand. Make an agreement with yourself to put distracting thoughts aside. Concentrate on what you see and hear.

Comprehension. This involves understanding vocabulary, language, and the key points the other person is making. If there's a language barrier, listening may be interrupted at this stage. When acronyms or buzzwords aren't clear to everyone, your message will get lost or corrupted. It's a good practice to paraphrase your understanding from time to time instead of making assumptions.

Interpretation. This is a higher level of understanding. At this stage, you as a listener are required to make inferences or judgments. Communication breakdowns often occur due to misunderstandings. It's important to separate facts from inferences. Ask yourself, "What are the facts?" "Am I making an assumption?"

Retention. You can attend to what's being said, understand it, and evaluate it, but if you don't retain the information, you'll lose the message. To increase your listening retention, take short notes to jog your memory. Use repetition. Repeat points to yourself mentally. You can also regroup or categorize material. As you listen, organize the information, mentally or on paper, into common groupings. This will help you retrieve it more easily. You can also

Listening is hard work. It's a skill that requires an investment of your time, but it pays off over the long term. Go back to the four aspects of good listening and identify the areas where you need work:

Exercise

- Attention,
- Comprehension,
- Interpretation, and
- Retention.

  What will you do to improve in each of these areas?

1. _____

2. _____

3. _____

4. _____

use mnemonics to create associations that will help you recall the information. This is good technique for remembering names.

What Is Your LQ (Listening Quotient)?

You've learned about the four aspects of good listening. Now let's evaluate how well you listen. Do the following self-assessment inventory to determine your LQ—your "Listening Quotient." For each statement, put a check mark in the appropriate column:

	Always	Sometimes	Rarely
1. I only listen for the facts.			
2. I take extensive notes.			
3. I tune out when I'm bored.			
4. I critique the speaker's style.			
5. I'm easily distracted.			
6. I react emotionally to words.			

Always Sometimes Rarely

7. I interrupt the speaker.

8. I rehearse my answers
    mentally.

9. I try to listen when I'm
    busy doing other things.

10. I answer the other person
     before checking
     my understanding.

Give yourself a 5 for every *always*, an 8 for every *sometimes*, and a 10 for every *rarely* response.

Scoring

- Above 90—You're an effective listener.
- 80-90—You listen well most of the time, but you could benefit from more training and practice.
- Below 80—You need to take a listening course and continue to work on this vital skill.

The Benefits of Listening

As a presenter and communicator, you'll benefit from being a good listener in several ways. You will:

- Have happier relationships,
- Increase your career success,
- Make fewer mistakes,
- Feel less stress, and
- Have more peace of mind.

Studies conducted by Professor Larry Barker in 1981 determined that college students spent 53% of their time in listening activities. Managers and executives spend even more time listening; in fact, most of their time is devoted to listening.

Yet most people don't listen well. If you don't believe that people don't listen well, try this experiment.

Next time you go to a coffee shop, ask for decaf tea. See what you get. I guarantee that you'll get coffee. Why? Because as soon as your server hears decaf, he or she will stop listening. The word "decaf" has become associated with *coffee*. One man I know shared a similar experience. Each morning, he and his wife would order "two black coffees." Invariably they would be asked, "Milk and sugar?"

There are two major reasons why people don't listen well: because most of us aren't trained to listen well, and because it requires putting the other person first. Most of us don't want to suspend our own egos long enough to truly listen.

Myths about Listening

We've all grown up believing certain myths about listening. Here are some of the most common myths.

1. We already know how to listen. No, we don't. We haven't been trained. Listening is a skill, not an instinct—and skills improve with practice. The schools are teaching backwards. Here's how we spend our time communicating: listening—53%, speaking—16%, reading—17%, writing—14%. But the schools train students in the following order—writing, reading, speaking—and devote little or no time to listening. Listening is last on the educational priority list but the most frequently used skill. We need to be trained how to listen well.

2. Listening is a passive, soft skill. The truth is that listening is an active skill that has real bottom-line results. Hearing is passive. It takes concentration to listen. Your heart beats faster and your body temperature rises when you actively listen. Corporations such as Sperry and American Airlines have saved money by improving their employees' listening skills. In one case at American Airlines, a first-class flight attendant noticed that people weren't eating olives on their salads. She told management.

They listened and stopped ordering olives. Nobody complained. The airline saved $40,000 a year by listening to one employee suggestion!

3. The deaf cannot listen. People who are deaf listen with their eyes. They're so tuned in to nonverbal communication that they can pick up nuances of behavior that the average person misses. Listening is not one-dimensional. It's multi-sensory. You need your eyes, ears, and emotions to listen well.

4. You can will yourself to listen. Can you will yourself to give a good speech if you've never practiced or been trained in public speaking? No. The same is true for listening. Listening is a skill. You can't simply will yourself to do something you don't know how to do. You may will yourself to pay attention, but it takes more than that to be a skilled listener.

5. Speaking is more vital to communication. What good is speaking if there are no ears to hear what you're saying? Most people don't like speaking in a vacuum. The success of any communication depends on both the speaker and the listener. The two skills must be interwoven. The speaker and the listener are interdependent.

Barriers to Listening

Now that we've examined some myths of listening, let's explore the barriers to listening:

Childhood messages. What messages did you receive as a child? "Children should be seen and not heard." "Speak when spoken to." "Get the wax out of your ears." These early messages color the way you listen today. If you heard, "Speak when spoken to," you probably listen passively, without interrupting others. A good listener, however, asks questions and clarifies information.

Identify the childhood messages you received. How do they help or hinder you?

1. _____

2. _____

Exercise

Assumptions. Read the following statement:

PARIS IN THE

THE SPRING

Did you read "Paris in the Spring"? Read it again. It says "Paris in the the Spring"—the word "the" appears twice. You assumed the sentence was written correctly. You filled in what logically made sense.

We all make assumptions. But when we don't validate our assumptions, we fail to listen to the speaker's message. This causes miscommunication. Don't assume you know what the audience wants. Ask people beforehand. In a one-to-one presentation, check your understanding.

I've had many chances to learn this lesson firsthand. One time, when my term as president of the New York chapter of the National Speakers Association was over, I met with the incoming president to orient her. Nancy and I agreed to meet before the board meeting, which was in a Manhattan hotel. Nancy said she would meet me at the restaurant at 3 o'clock. This would give us two hours together.

The restaurant was an open area that looked out onto the lobby. I arrived fifteen minutes early, so I found an empty room and did some work. At 3 o'clock, I walked out to the lobby, looked in the restaurant, and didn't see Nancy. It was still early, so I went back to the room, only to return at 3:15. Again I looked around. Nancy wasn't by the door and she wasn't seated in the restaurant. I figured there was a lot of traffic and that she'd be arriving soon.

I scanned the lobby and restaurant again at 3:30 and at 3:45. Still no Nancy. Now I was concerned. I called Nancy's home but nobody answered. At 4 o'clock, I came out again, this time walking the entire length of the lobby to the entrance. As I walked back I heard my name. It was Nancy. She'd been seated in the back of the restaurant at a table that wasn't easily visible. She'd been there since 3 o'clock!

What happened? I'd made an assumption that Nancy would wait for me at the restaurant before being seated. She in turn assumed that I would give her name to the waiter so that he would bring me to her table. "At the restaurant" had different meanings for both of us. I'd also assumed that if Nancy were seated, she would sit in an easily visible seat. Nancy did have visibility. She had a clear view of the lobby entrance. Unfortunately, I had arrived early. We both assumed that the other person was late.

What assumptions do you make as a speaker? Do you assume that the audience speaks your language? When you use buzzwords and jargon, do you bother to define the terms? Do you assume that the meeting room will meet your specifications? Or do you ask to see the room and provide a checklist for your audio-visual requirements? When someone in the audience asks a question, do you assume you know what he or she means. Or do you clarify your understanding?

Emotions. Listening decreases as emotions increase. To listen well, we need to be in a calm state of mind. Do your audience members look fearful or angry? Then they aren't fully present to listen in the moment. Don't keep talking at them. Discover the reason for those emotions or do something to break the negative pattern. Try humor. It's difficult to feel fear or anger when you're laughing.

Your job as a presenter is to create a safe, pleasant atmosphere where people can listen. As a presenter, you must have control of your own emotions. When an audience challenges you or looks

Here's an exercise to identify your emotional triggers.
Make a list of any words, statements, or facial expressions (e.g.,
rolling eyes, frowning, crossed arms, etc.) that will trigger
your emotions:

1. _____

2. _____

What feelings do these words or actions trigger in you?

1. _____

2 _____

What will you do the next time you encounter these triggers?

1. _____

2. _____

Exercise

bored or skeptical, don't take it personally. When you know what
triggers your emotions, you'll have greater control over yourself.

Making judgments. Most of us listen to what we want to hear.
We can easily tune out when we don't like the message or the
messenger. How often do you discount what you hear because the
speaker is boring, unappealing, unstylish, or controversial? Listen
to the messages inside your head. If you're critiquing the speaker,
you aren't listening. By the same token, if you're critiquing or
judging the audience, you're not listening either. You cannot truly
listen with an internal dialogue going on inside you.

By judging the audience, you put your relationship with them
at risk. Your judgments may be premature.

A consultant I know once told a story about a salesperson who
came to his office to sell the consultant his services. In the middle
of the conversation, the salesperson said, "Forget it. It's obvious
you're not interested." The consultant was startled: "What do you

mean? I'm very interested. Where did you get that impression?" The salesperson said, "Well, you're sitting there with your arms folded." That just happened to be the consultant's listening posture. Don't be quick to judge.

Rehearsing your responses. If you're thinking of your next response to what someone is saying, you aren't present in the moment. Rather, you're in the future—you're not truly listening.

This is most obvious during question-and-answer sessions. The speaker is so concerned about giving the correct answer that he or she scans ahead, searching for the right response.

In one-to-one presentations or sales calls, listening is especially critical. If you rehearse your answers in these situations, you'll sound canned. So clear your mind and listen to the entire message. Then you can respond.

Distractions. Distractions are one of the major reasons we don't listen. Distractions can be internal (e.g., your own thoughts about the day's activities, worrying about loved ones, and so one) or external (e.g., noise, poor lighting, too much clutter, and so on).

If you're talking to someone, he or she will likely turn to look briefly at another person who walks into the room. That is an external distraction.

You may have no control over environmental distractions, but you can control your reaction to them. You can learn to tune out background noise. When someone walks into the room, make a bet with yourself that you won't look up. Instead, continue to listen. It may seem difficult at first, but this is just a bad habit you must break.

If competing thoughts are your challenge, try this technique: each time your mind wanders, say to yourself, "Pay attention." Eventually you'll listen more and be distracted less.

Fatigue. It's difficult to listen when you're tired. If fatigue is a problem for you, get enough rest the night before your presentation. Eat well and avoid high-sugar snacks, which will cause your energy to crash.

Exercise

Write down some of your common internal and external distractions:

Internal

1. _____

2. _____

External (e.g., noise, poor lighting, too much clutter, etc.)

1. _____

2. _____

Action Plan (What will you do to change how you react to distrations?)

1. _____

2. _____

As the speaker, you can energize yourself by taking breaks. A good rule of thumb is to break every hour for five or ten minutes. Move around and get your audience to move as well. Ask them to stand. Create a two-minute exercise, and ask people to talk to their partner. Your job is to energize them so that they can listen.

Staring at visual aids for any length of time can tire the eyes. Shut off the overhead at intervals. If you're tired, your audience will be too. Find that fire in the belly. Change your voice. Get excited. Move your body and get the energy going.

Excessive notetaking. Writing a few notes definitely helps the listening process. You can get into trouble, however, if you take copious notes. You can't write down every word the speaker is saying and expect to hear the message. Some students are so accustomed to taking notes that if the professor says, "Good morning," they write it down. When you see the audience members taking extensive notes, test their listening by making an odd statement. For example: "If your parents didn't have children, you probably won't either." Or, "After the crash they buried the survivors in the woods." If you don't get a chuckle, it's time to take a break.

Listening only for facts. If you do this, you may get the facts but miss the message.

Suppose a speaker is giving a speech about President Kennedy. You learn that no matter how exhausted Kennedy was, and that even though he suffered from back problems, he swam and persisted and saved many men by never giving up. The speaker also mentions that Kennedy's boat was PT 109. Your friend asks you afterward, "How was the speech?" You reply, "Did you know that Kennedy's boat was PT 109?" Your friend says, "So what? What was the point of the speech?" You focused on an unimportant detail and missed the important point of perseverance.

Facts alone do not convey the message. Listen for main themes and ideas.

Poor posture. Physiology can affect your mental state. Imagine how people who are depressed look. They're slumped, they tend to look down, and they move slowly. Your posture has an impact on your listening behavior. A good listener is alert and looks at the speaker. A speaker who listens well looks directly at individuals in the audience. Slouching communicates poor listening. So stand or sit up straight.

Three Levels of Listening

Consider where you are on the "Listening Ladder." The Listening Ladder has three rungs, or levels: sporadic, surface, and active listening.

Level 3 is *sporadic listening*. This is also known as faking it. If you're a sporadic listener, you tune in and tune out. You're aware of others but you're paying attention to yourself. If the person you're with asks a question, you may not be able to answer because you weren't really listening. You listen only long enough for the other person to have a chance to talk. This is called listening to respond. You have little concern for real understanding.

Level 2 is *surface listening*. If you're a surface listener, you hear the surface words and content, but you miss the emotion. This is the Mr. Spock syndrome: you, the listener, are having a logical experience, but chances are you're missing main points and the message because you don't hear the speaker's intent. Surface listeners seem emotionally detached and may not participate in the interaction. If you're a surface listener, you risk being involved in misunderstandings with other people. The people you interact with may believe that you're receiving the messages they're sending.

Level 1 is *active listening*. This is your goal If you're an active listener, you're tuned into feelings and content. You engage in multi-sensory listening—that is, listening with your eyes, ears, and emotions. You observe body language, you tune into tone of voice, and you empathize with feelings and intent. You don't judge the speaker but instead listen with an open mind. You also participate actively, with both your words and your nonverbal actions.

Listening and You, the Presenter

Your job as a presenter is twofold: to listen to your audience and to help your audience listen to you. Here are some of the major reasons why your audience may not be listening to what you're saying:

- Your speech is too long.
- Your speech is disjointed.
- Your speech is inaudible. You may speak too fast or too softly,

or maybe there's too much background noise.
- You're boring.
- Your speech is boring.
- You lack passion—you don't believe in your message.

Research demonstrates that audience members are poor listeners, generally speaking. As a speaker, you have 20 seconds to grab people's attention. If you get their attention, they'll stay with you for eight to ten minutes. You must then change your style for two to three minutes; if you do, the audience will stay with you for another eight to ten minutes.

Why are these numbers significant?

This listening pattern exactly matches the TV sitcom formula. Audiences are programmed from years of watching television. When you present, you're competing with standards and expectations set by television.

With that in mind, the key to grabbing and maintaining attention is BVE: brevity, variety, and entertainment.

Watch a few TV commercials and shows. You'll see some interesting similarities. Messages are delivered in sound bites—short, concise phrases or sentences that pack a punch. Consider for example, the following company sound bites:
- "When it absolutely, positively has to be there overnight." (Federal Express)
- "We bring good things to light." (GE)
- "Just do it!" (Nike)
  Now consider these sound bites from motivational speakers:
- "See you at the top." (Zig Ziglar)
- "You've got to be hungry." (Les Brown)
- "If it is to be it is up to me." (Dennis Waitley)

Brevity Breaks Boredom

Audiences will tune out on you if you overwhelm them with long, winding phrases and tedious details. Speak crisply and you'll help them stay active and alert. Practice speaking in sound bites. What memorable slogan or repetitive phrase can you create to help people keep listening to you?

Variety Adds Vitality

Once you've captured people's attention, introduce change. Switch gears. Change the topic. Do something different. Make a different point, or make the same point in a different way. Use a prop. Soften your voice to a whisper. Walk into the crowd. Use humor. Demonstrate your idea. Ask a question.

Listeners will drift in and out by nature. You can stimulate them by introducing variety.

Entertainment Engages

Don't forget the entertainment factor. It isn't enough to simply add variety. Audiences want to have fun. Remember the TV sit-coms. We're accustomed to being entertained. Imagine the disappointment of kids who enter kindergarten after a long relationship with Big Bird. The teachers can't compete with *Sesame Street* unless they make the message fun.

Adults too prefer to be entertained, not lectured. So add some spice and fun.
- Use humor.
- Introduce a brainteaser.
- Give people a challenge.
- Play music.
- Try a magic trick.
- Ask audience members to repeat a phrase.
- Ask for an audience volunteer.
- Create a short exercise and put people in pairs.
- Have your listeners fill in a worksheet.
- Show a quick video.
- Create a quiz.

Just get people involved! People listen longer and better when they're participating. Make your presentation an experience.

When Not to Listen

Most of us experience all three levels of the Listening Ladder in the course of a day or when we're listening to someone else's presentation. But knowing when *not* to listen is just as important as knowing how to listen well.

How do you know when it's best not to listen? Use the HALT approach: hungry, angry, lonely, or tired. If you are hungry, angry, lonely, or tired, it's best not to try to listen to someone else. These are all emotional states, and listening works best in the absence of intense emotion.

Another time when it's best not to listen is when you're busy. Instead of faking it, tell the person, "I just can't listen to you right now."

My husband used this strategy with me recently. After a trip to the supermarket, I was busy taking the food out of the bags and stocking the cabinet and refrigerator shelves. My husband was trying to have a conversation with me. I was obviously at Level 3 because I wasn't really paying attention to him. He noticed I wasn't completely present and said calmly, "I'll talk to you later when you have time to listen." I later thanked him because he was right: I hadn't been ready to listen.

Another situation in which it's best not to listen is when the other person is being abusive. Effective speakers can calm a hostile audience with empathetic listening. But if this isn't working for you, break off communication. Try again when audience members are more even-tempered.

Becoming a Better Listener

You can see how vital listening is to communication. You're not just giving a speech. You're listening to your audience, which may be a group, a customer, a student, an employee, a manager, a supplier, or a patient.

There are several strategies you can take to listen better to your audience members or other people in general:

1. **Get ready to listen.** Prepare yourself physically by eating well and getting rest the night before your talk. Mentally prepare yourself by clearing your mind of internal noise.
2. **Remove distractions.** Clear your desk of clutter. Hold all phone calls.
3. **Check the audio-visual equipment.** Close the blinds to prevent glare and close the door to shut out extraneous sounds.
4. **Keep an open mind.** Suspend judgment. Commit to accepting audience members' opinions even if you don't agree with them. Don't assume or jump to conclusions. You'll usually be wrong.
5. **Listen for main themes.** What points is the speaker making? What is the speaker's intent? Good listening involves main themes.
6. **Take short notes.** Keep a notepad handy and jot down major points. For large audiences, you can write concerns or comments on a flip chart or a transparency. This will help you remember the message. Be careful not to take so many notes that you don't hear the message.
7. **Control your emotions.** Know what sets you off. When your emotions are triggered, take five. Breathe. Ask to speak to the other person at a later time. You must have a clear head to listen.
8. **Allow the speaker to finish.** This applies whether you're in a one-to-one conversation or a formal question-and-answer period. Listening is a form of respect. Listen to the entire

message. If you have trouble allowing people to finish, keep a glass of water handy. That way, when you're tempted to interrupt, you can take a sip of water. To change a negative habit, you must replace it with a positive behavior.

9. **Listen for hidden messages.** Engage in multi-sensory listening. Listen with your eyes, ears, and emotions. What does the other person's body language tell you? What do you hear in his or her voice? What does your gut tell you? Are the person's words congruent with his or her body and voice? If you're speaking to a large audience, how attentive do they seem? Are their questions legitimate or are they designed to trap you? What is said in jest? (There may be a hidden agenda.)

10. **Ask questions**. Start with fact-finding questions to discover basic information. Then ask questions to uncover feelings. Continue to probe with follow-up questions. For example, if someone says, "Customers expect too much," continue to probe. "Which customers?" "What do you mean by 'expect too much'?" "What specifically do they expect?" "How do you know that?" Too often we listen superficially and accept the surface message. Good questioning leads to better listening. Better listening leads to the true message.

11. **Respond verbally and nonverbally.** Look at your audience. Really look—eye to eye, person to person. Stay with each person for a while. Nod, use facial expressions, and make statements to show you're listening. If as a speaker you truly listen to your audience, you demonstrate caring. Listening helps you build a relationship with your audience.

Tips to Help Your Audience Listen to You

1. **Have a conversation.** Use the word "you" throughout your talk. Use phrases such as "Ask yourself...," "What if we...," "What would you do if...," and "How many of you...." You'll

distance yourself from the audience by using formal, passive language.

2. **Get personal.** Put yourself into your speech. Tell listeners about your own experiences and stories. People relate better to personal experiences than to statistics. They want to know who you are and what you've lived through.

3. **Keep it current.** Listeners will be more attentive if you speak about today's events or tomorrow's meeting. If the topic is old news, people will start to drift.

4. **Speak in specifics.** Concrete information is more interesting than vague generalities. If you're talking about drug smuggling, don't talk about numbers. Talk about Mexico and Colombia. Give specific examples.

5. **Present with passion.** Pump up your voice, words, and energy. Enthusiasm is contagious. If you're excited about your message and you vary your voice, your audience will stay alert. If you're a monotone, your listeners will tune out.

6. **Get physical.** Some of the top speakers really work the room. You don't have to be dramatic, but moving from one part of the platform to another causes a shift in attention. If you stay glued behind the lectern, you'll struggle to engage your listeners. Don't be afraid to step out from behind the lectern to tell a story. This will immediately stimulate attention.

7. **Frame it in the familiar.** The audience won't stay with you if your material is too complex. Use analogies, examples, and metaphors to make things easier to understand. A telecommunications techie compared the Internet to a wide cardboard tube. He said the tube was the bandwidth, or how much data could get through. He placed a small soda bottle into the open tube. It went through easily. He said the soda bottle represented text. Then he took a large detergent bottle and barely squeezed it through the opening. The laundry bottle represented graphics. Graphics take up a lot more memory and space and download more slowly. By using the

familiar, this presenter helped his audience understand.

8. **Involve the audience.** Ask people to be part of your demonstration by coming up on stage to assist you. Or, ask them to supply information. They can fill in the blanks by shouting out answers or by writing them down. They can also come up with their own ideas. For example, ask audience members to choose three types of ethnic foods. People can call out suggestions and you can use the first three you hear.

Checklist for Listening

DO

- **Get ready physically and mentally.** Listening is a skill. Get ready by physically removing distractions. If you're listening to a one-to-one presentation, clear your desk of clutter and hold phone calls. If you're speaking in a larger room, close the back door and draw the drapes. Concentrate on the audience and don't let your mind wander.
- **Look at the speaker or the audience.** It's difficult to listen if you don't focus your eyes. Look at the individual or the audience so that you can listen to nonverbals. During questions and answers, look directly at the questioner. This is a sign of respect.
- **Take notes.** For one-to-one meetings, jot down a few notes to jog your memory. But don't overdo it. If you're constantly writing, you'll lose your concentration.
- **Keep an open mind.** Be willing to consider new ideas. You can conclude at the end of the session that you disagree with the person or with the audience based on the evidence. But unless you begin with an open mind, you won't truly listen to others. Instead, you'll be listening to your own thoughts.
- **Clarify and ask questions.** In one-to-one conversations, ask questions to clarify the meaning: "Can you elaborate?" "What

do you mean?" "What makes you say that?"

- **Check back for understanding.** Paraphrase what the person says before you respond. This ensures that you really understand. It also shows you care.
- **Listen to understand.** Most people listen to respond. They listen until they can find a pause where they can jump in with their opinion. Listening to understand means that you suspend your ego and concentrate on the other person's message.
- **Keep your emotions in check.** Listening takes a nosedive when emotions are high. If you're in a highly emotional state, take a break and offer to listen later.
- **Mentally summarize.** Your brain can process almost four times faster than you can speak and twice as fast as you can listen. No wonder our minds wander! Instead of tuning out, mentally summarize the other person's main points. This will keep you listening and concentrating.
- **Understand how to listen.** The four steps to listening are attending, comprehending, interpreting, and retaining. If you have difficulty in any of these areas, practice.

DON'T

- **Jump to conclusions.** It's so easy to make inferences instead of hearing what was really said. Listen before you leap. Ask yourself, "Is that a fact or an inference?" Ask questions to check out your assumptions.
- **Interrupt.** This is rude behavior and it signals that you aren't listening. Let the person finish before you respond. When you're tempted to interrupt, take a sip of water instead. If you think you'll forget your thought, write it down.
- **Judge the speaker.** You may not like the speakers style, but you can still listen. If you're critiquing the speaker's delivery or dress, you're not listening. When you catch yourself critiquing, stop. Then focus once again on the message.
- **Advise.** Listening is not giving advice. Most people want you to listen because they need to vent. If they want your advice,

they'll ask for it. People talk to relieve their anxiety. Most people will be able to solve their own problems.

- **Listen when you're tired.** Let people know when you're tired
  and offer to listen later. Don't pretend you're listening when
  you're not.

Part 3. Structure & Organization

Research and Analyze Your Audience

To sell John Brown what John Brown buys, you've
got to see things through John Brown's eyes.
–David J. Schwartz, Ph.D.

What's the first step in preparing your presentation? Before you begin your research, there's a critical task you must do—a task that many speakers overlook or take lightly. Step one is knowing your audience.

Let me illustrate why this is such a critical step to your speaking success. Suppose your topic was New York City restaurants.

You're told the audience is a group of upscale, sophisticated tourists. What would you emphasize in your speech? Cuisine? Ambiance? Location? Chef? Wine list? Celebrities? Snob appeal?

What if you learned that your audience was going to be fifth-graders in a local school? Now you would highlight fast food, McDonald's, prizes, coupons, entertainment, and fun.

You would present on the same topic but give two entirely different speeches. Imagine how disastrous it would be to give the first presentation to the fifth-graders. Yet this happens all the time. The speech you gave in your company failed when you gave it to your customers or suppliers. The rousing applause you received from the men's group turned to icy indifference when you spoke to the women's club. All because you didn't take time to consider your audience.

A man was once talking to a professional association about a new assessment instrument that measures communication skills. Everyone at the conference was interested, and the speaker attracted some of the senior members of the industry to his presentation. He proceeded to use a sports analogy. Then he used a second sports analogy. And a third sports analogy. Finally, a woman raised her hand and asked, "How does this work with women?" The presenter realized that he had overused sports examples.

If you forget to consider the makeup of your audience, you risk losing them. So let's begin this discussion by helping you understand the types of audiences you will have.

Types of Audiences: Generalist vs. Specialist

Audiences can be grouped into two major categories: generalist and specialist.

Generalist audience. This group is mixed. It's the public at large. Think about a seminar that is advertised in a college catalog or direct-mail brochure. Anyone can sign up. There may be a wide age range, a variety of occupations, differing levels of knowledge and experience, and many geographical origins among audience members. This is one of the most challenging audiences because of the disparity in backgrounds. Their expectations may differ widely. When you're speaking to this type of group, you'll have to work hard to meet their needs and to speak at the right level.

Specialist audience. This audience is a subgroup of a general population. It may be the sales department of your company or the account executives of an ad agency. It could be the members of a professional association such as the Rotary, the garden club, an entrepreneurs' group, or the dental association. Or you may be speaking to high school or college students.

Members of this audience have a common link of belonging to a group, organization, or profession. Specialist audiences can be broad or narrow in scope. A broad specialist group could be a company meeting of all employees. The employees are from different departments but they all belong to the same company, and the message will be the same for all. A narrower specialist audience might be a meeting for all programmers in the MIS department. The message would be more technical in nature and specific to that group. In many cases, it's easier to analyze and plan for a specialist audience.

Special Audiences: Superiors, Peers, Direct Reports, Teen Groups, and Multicultural Audiences

Although there are some commonalties among certain groups or levels, not all audiences are alike. Here are some special audiences to consider, along with some simple guidelines for presenting effectively to each.

Executives or superiors. When addressing senior management or your superiors, be careful about how you position your recommendations. Suggest, don't tell. They will not like you dictating to them. Back up your ideas with facts and talk in terms of what is important to them. Make your presentation more formal and to the point. Senior managers usually want the executive summary. They want to know what you're recommending, what your plan is, what the result will be, and how much will it cost. They don't want the nitty-gritty details. But be prepared in case they do ask for them.

Executives can be a tough group. They expect you to be up to date, well-organized, and confident. Heated debates may arise because of in-house power plays. Don't get in the middle. Let them handle it. Your job is to present the data.

Peer group. If you're talking to your co-workers or other people at your level, share information and relate to them on their level. You can be less formal with your peers and can easily involve them. Credit them when appropriate and ask for their input: "Sue, you reduced turnover. Could you tell us how you did it?" By asking for their input, you'll gain their support and respect.

Direct reports or subordinates. With people at a more junior level, details are important. These are the people who will be implementing the ideas, so demonstrations and examples will be important. If you're explaining how to process claims, have examples that people can take back with them. Be specific. Repeat your main points. If appropriate, ask people to explain their understanding of the procedure.

Teen groups. You may be called upon to speak to youth groups in your community. If you're accustomed to adult audiences, you're in for a surprise when presenting to teens. Working with young people can be very rewarding. At the same time, if you're not prepared, teens can be a very tough audience. Adults may applaud politely. If teenagers don't like your speech, they tend to me more vocal. They're not afraid to say, "This stinks!" (And that's the edited version.)

To succeed in presenting to teens, here are some guidelines to consider:

1. Teens expect to be entertained.
2. They often have short attention spans. You must hook them in the first thirty seconds.
3. They are easily influenced by their peer group and will follow the leader. There is a strong need to be accepted. You must know how to gain control and protect anyone whose self-esteem is being challenged by the group.
4. Teenagers may challenge your authority. You may not get assistance from the adult leaders. Ask how they want you to handle disruptions during your presentation.
5. Teens can be cynical, sophisticated, and distrusting. You must prove your sincerity.
6. Teenagers can be self-absorbed. They want to know, "What's in it for me?" Sell them on the benefits of listening to you. Use their examples. Play their music.
7. Teens are direct with their opinions. You may need to develop a thick skin. Don't take comments personally. The good news is that you'll know where you stand with them.
8. Teenagers want to feel a sense of control. Don't talk at them. Involve them through interactive activities.
9. Teens resent being talked down to. Respect their opinions. Don't ask baby questions. Listen attentively and don't let your opinions get in the way.
10. Teens are easily bored. Pace your presentation. Vary your voice.
11. Create excitement. Get them moving.
12. Give them how-to's, not should's. Teens don't want you to preach. But they do appreciate practical tips. Teens often know right from wrong. What they don't know is how to do something, whether it be communicating, filling out a job application, or resolving conflicts.

13. Teens are often poor listeners. Make your presentation visual. Use props. Create pictures with your language. Use repetition and games to aid understanding and memory.

It may take some time to get teens involved. Don't panic if they don't raise their hands or respond to your questions immediately. Once you gain their trust and respect, speaking to teenagers can be a wonderful, rewarding experience.

Multicultural audiences. In today's world, our neighbors, colleagues, customers, and audiences can be from just about any corner of the globe. Consider this warning from Hilka Klinkenberg, international etiquette and protocol expert and author of the book, *At Ease Professionally* (1992): "These days, virtually any general audience anywhere in America is multicultural. Speakers who do not put their programs together with this consideration in mind risk failure." Speaking to multicultural audiences requires greater sensitivity. When speaking to multicultural audiences, keep these tips in mind:

1. Asians generally don't like to answer direct questions. They also don't like being singled out or called upon as volunteers. This doesn't mean you should lecture the entire time. Keep the audience's interest by developing interactive exercises in which members can discuss points with a partner. Have participants write down points or engage in reading exercises.

2. Create a positive perception as the presenter. Be formal at first and test the group. It's better to maintain your authority initially in order to earn their respect. The very casual, touchy-feely approach may not be well received. Strive to create a relationship first.

3. Some cultures may require copious details, sources, and data. You will gain credibility by stating your educational credentials and experience up front. Inundate the audience members with the information they need and be prepared to support what you say with hard evidence and examples.

4. Be aware of status levels. Don't group managers and secre-

taries together. Americans tend to be more egalitarian than most cultures. And be sure your stories and illustrations reflect the appropriate status level.

5. Be careful about identifying mistakes. This is especially true if you're speaking to Asians, who generally need to save face. If someone in this type of audience answers your question incorrectly, ask, "Could you explain that?" or "What led you to your conclusion?" Find a point where you can agree.

6. Avoid self-defeating behaviors. When one instructor didn't get answers to his direct questions, he got louder and louder. Don't continue the behavior that's causing the problem. If audience members don't respond to your questions, try something else. Remember the definition of insanity—doing the same thing over and over again and expecting a different result!

7. Know how different cultures perceive your ethnicity. Japanese people may perceive Americans as too aggressive, while Europeans may find Americans superficial and overly friendly.

8. Don't make assumptions about individuals from different cultures. Remember that people have different personalities within their cultures. For example, not all Asians are shy. The Japanese may not like being asked direct questions, while the Chinese do. Some Asians may be reticent to talk. Latin Americans are very verbal and need ample opportunities to discuss and express themselves. Research cultural differences to understand your audience.

9. Be careful with humor. Telling jokes is risky business even with a mixed audience. Listeners probably won't understand the joke and you risk offending people as well. If you're speaking overseas, avoid humor altogether. People in the audience are unlikely to get it. American humor doesn't even translate to a British audience.

10. Avoid using idioms unless you explain the expression. Be

aware that Americans use a lot of sports and business analogies, such as "hit all the bases," "bigger bang for the buck," and "Monday morning quarterback." Multicultural audiences won't understand what you mean by these expressions.

11. Speak slowly and articulate carefully. Even fluent speakers need additional time to process another language. Repeat instructions two or three times. Check for nonverbal signs of misunderstanding.

12. Realize that audience members may lack confidence in their English skills. Give them extra time to respond to your questions or statements.

13. Use visual aids. Visuals help your listeners understand and retain your message. But the visuals must be ethnically appropriate and diverse. If you're speaking to a male audience in an Arab country, you would not have women represented in your slides or overheads.

14. Give people more time to read visual aids and handouts. Americans tend to skim information, while Japanese audiences may bring dictionaries and look up every word.

15. Be sensitive to gender issues. Women may not be accepted as presenters in certain cultures, such as Saudi Arabia. This doesn't mean that you should abdicate your position. It does mean, however, that you need to be aware of the inherent resistance and establish your credibility.

Speaking Overseas

When you're invited to speak overseas, your presentation will be in English unless you speak the other language like a native. You may lack the nuances of the language, which become important in a formal presentation—especially in the absence of verbal feedback. You won't know if silence means interest or confusion.

It's a good idea, however, to say a few words in the foreign language. It shows good will and caring. Learn a couple of greetings or phrases in their language and you will go a long way in developing rapport. This works best at the beginning of the presentation, when you have to grab people's attention.

Be sure to write the statement down and practice it out loud beforehand. You don't want to use the wrong words or, worse, insult anyone. This is especially true in the Chinese language, in which a shift in intonation can totally change the meaning of what you say.

Remember that *I Love Lucy* episode in which Lucy meets her Cuban relatives for the first time? Lucy wants to impress them by saying a few words in Spanish. She means to greet Ricky's uncle with "mucho gusto" (it's a pleasure), but she mispronounces it as "mucha grassa." The uncle becomes very insulted. Ricky then informs Lucy that she has just called the man fat.

While you're practicing the language, do your homework on the culture as well. For instance, in the U.S., we consider ourselves Americans, but so do people in South America, who consider us North Americans. Also, be cognizant of gestures. The gesture of the index finger and thumb forming a circle with three upright fingers means "A-OK" in the U.S. But in Brazil, that same gesture is an obscenity. "Don't just rehearse the words, choreograph every gesture so that you don't slip up," advises Hilka Klinkenberg, president of Etiquette International. "Even something as simple as putting your hands in your pocket while addressing a European audience can alienate your listeners."

Before you go abroad, talk to a colleague who has spoken in that country. Most professional speakers will tell you that they research and prepare much longer when they're going to be speaking overseas. Talk to your contact person and ask for coaching on the culture. Find books and videos on international protocol. Speak to your librarian. Write to the foreign consulate. Check the Internet. Be prepared. Good sources of information are the books, *Kiss, Bow, or Shake Hands* (1996) and *At Ease Professionally* (1992), both by Hilka Klinkenberg.

Translation Tips

When you use an interpreter for your presentation, think through the process before diving in. Don't assume that your audience is fluent in English. There may be differing levels of proficiency among the audience members.

When using an interpreter, here are some tips to consider:

1. *Speak to the audience, not to the interpreter*. It's easy to forget your audience, especially if your presentation is at a business meeting.

2. *Determine if the interpretation will be simultaneous or consecutive*. Simultaneous interpretation is used at the United Nations. The presenter speaks and the interpreter interprets at the same time. The listeners may use headsets to hear the language of their choice. Consecutive interpretation means that you speak first and when you finish your sentence, the interpreter interprets. The reason this is important is it will affect whether you can give the talk as you normally would or whether you have to plan how much to say before you pause for translation.

3. *Speak in sound bites*. Use short sentences and lots of pauses. For example, "Good morning. (pause) Today I'm going to talk about (pause) the importance of business planning."

4. *Meet with the interpreter in advance*. Explain your material and the concepts you'll be presenting. Give the interpreter a copy of your written speech. You can still ad-lib, but this will help the interpreter understand your purpose and content.

5. *Determine where the interpreter studied English*. Choose someone who studied in the United States. British English is different, and an interpreter with this background may have difficulty with American idioms.

6. *Explain the meaning of idioms and expressions in advance*. One speaker told her audience that when her husband didn't want her to go to Russia, she told him, "Too bad, I'm going

anyway." The interpreter would not interpret it. In the interpreter's culture, "too bad" meant wishing someone much badness.

7. *Learn about the culture in advance.* There were two reasons the interpreter in the example above would not translate the "too bad" statement. One reason was semantic. The other reason was cultural. For a woman to tell her husband that she would go on a trip without his consent was a statement of equality and assertiveness. That would be unacceptable for a Russian woman to do.

8. *Define terms.* Don't assume that people will understand the terms you'll be using in your speech. Clarify terms by citing specific examples when you introduce new concepts. For example, the business concept of quality control and consistency of products may be different to the interpreter. An American speaker explained that consistency meant the ability to reproduce a product exactly so that there would be no variations in color, shape, texture, size, etc. At that point, the interpreter turned to the speaker and said, "Oh, I thought consistency meant durability."

9. *Trust your gut.* If the audience isn't responding the way you thought they would, chances are your message isn't getting across very well. This is especially true with humor. Don't be afraid to check back with your interpreter to ensure understanding. Ask for advice.

Developing a Listener Profile

In assessing your audience, you first consider whether you'll be speaking to a specialist or generalist group. You then take into consideration any special audience characteristics, as described above.

The next step is to begin creating a listener profile. Consider everything you would ideally like to know about your audience. Here are some areas to consider:

Size. How large is the group? Is it a handful of people at a meeting or an auditorium of 700 listeners? The principles are the same for small and large groups, though you will need to make some minor adjustments for each type of group. For example, it may make a difference in the kind of visuals you use.

Age. What is the average age of audience members? Age is a consideration when you're planning the types of examples and humor you're going to use and choosing the medium you'll be using. You aren't going to use video clips from MTV for a senior audience. For a financial presentation, investment goals will be different for young professionals vs. retirees. If there is a wide disparity in age, you'll have a greater challenge to meet everyone's needs.

Gender. Are you speaking to a gender-mixed group? What is the male-to-female ratio? Addressing a mixed group is different from addressing a single-sex audience. If the audience is all male, you can use more sports analogies and allusions to things males might have experienced. In a female group, you can get more sentimental, with more mentions of the family, for example.

Knowledge. What do audience members already know about your topic? What don't they know? What do they most need to know? These questions will help you focus your remarks. If people already know the basics, you must add greater value. If people don't know much about the subject, you must be careful not to talk over their heads—without being too simplistic. Separate the nice-to-knows from the need-to-knows. If time is an issue, what would be the most important points to make?

Education. What is the formal education of the audience members? Are they high school graduates? Do they have advanced degrees? Are there literacy issues? The formal education level of your audience will determine the types of handouts to prepare, how much text versus visuals to use, the size of the typeface you use in your handouts, and the examples you'll be using. Don't assume that everyone can read and write.

Experience. One can have knowledge of a subject without experience. Audience members may hold MBAs, but how long have they been managing people? Have they managed a department? In a large corporation or a small business? For how long? Are there varying levels of experience in the group?

Level. What are the levels or titles of the group members? Are supervisors together with their direct reports? Is it an entry-level group or senior management? What do people's titles really mean? Who has power of position and who has real power or influence?

Job responsibilities. What do audience members do in their jobs? What challenges do they face? On whom do they depend for information? Whom do they serve? What are the recent trends in their industry? Who are their competitors?

Regional background. Where are audience members from? Are they local or from out-of-state? If you're addressing Southerners, speak more slowly. When you're speaking to New Yorkers, keep a quick pace. If you're speaking out of town, read the local paper and use current events and expressions from the region. Take time to enunciate carefully and slowly if your accent is different. This is especially critical with foreign audiences. If the audience includes foreigners, identify the countries people are from. Determine the level of English proficiency.

Political affiliations. Who in the audience reports to whom? Who has the top person's ear? Who is able to influence decisions? What are the politics of this group or organization? Are people approachable? Do they value formality? Who is the decision-maker? (This is especially important when you're giving persuasive presentations.)

Socioeconomic background. Are you speaking to working-class audience members who are trying to make ends meet? Then don't recommend a $5,000 solution. If your audience is primarily upscale, people won't be interested in learning shopping tips for Wal-Mart. Knowing the social and economic background of audience members will help you speak their language—and it may save you embarrassment as well.

Hidden agendas. What hidden motives could there be for attending or setting up this meeting or presentation? What needs beyond the obvious or stated ones could there be for your presentation? For example, if you were asked to speak about change, does the organization really want to change, or is it just trying to improve its image? When you encounter resistance toward your topic, it may be due to motives of which you are unaware. This is usually true of a few individuals rather than the entire audience.

Attitude. How do audience members feel about your topic? Do they like and respect the subject? Is there a general interest in it, or do people resent having to hear your message? It's critical to know what you're walking into. It's wonderful to have a receptive audience. But if they're going to be hostile, you had better be prepared for it.

Image. What is the organization's image? How does the organization describe itself? What is its philosophy or style? How do people in the organization dress? Make sure your style is appropriate for the group.

Goals, expectations, and needs. It's absolutely critical to know the following before preparing your talk:

- What are the goals of the audience members? Why did they ask you to speak? To improve morale? To motivate people and shake them up? To improve team building or people's knowledge bases?

- What do audience members expect of you as a speaker? To understand their business? To know the audience personally? To be entertaining? To be an expert? To dazzle them with visuals?
- What do people need to make this presentation a success? Extra time? Flexibility? Follow-up? Handouts?

You can answer these questions by talking to the meeting planner or the person who invited you to speak.

Use the "Listener Profile" shown on pages 124 and 125 to analyze your audience. You should do this before every presentation you make.

If you analyze your audience ahead of time, you'll increase your success and avoid embarrassment and frustration. If you don't, you risk being the right messenger with the wrong message. The Listener Profile ensures that you are the right messenger with the right message!

Today's Audience Culture

If you look at the most common trends, you can make some general statements about today's audiences:

They're busy. Most people are pressed for time. They're juggling activities—jobs, school, children. They have less administrative help at work but are expected to produce twice as much. As a result, people are in a hurry and can grow impatient. If you take too long to make your point or don't grab their attention quickly, they'll walk out on you—mentally and perhaps physically!

They're sophisticated. Audiences are exposed to higher levels of entertainment and technology. With desktop publishing and multimedia, they can produce their own graphics and slide presentations. They'll expect your visual presentation to be of high quality. You cannot photocopy a black-and-white page onto an overhead and expect to be viewed as professional. People will be discon-

Listener Profile

Name of company/association/department _____

Purpose of meeting/presentation _____

(Why do they want you to speak? e.g., annual sales meeting, monthly department update)

Goals, expectations, and needs (of the meeting planner, contact person, and/or the audience)—e.g., do they expect humor? a slide show? an active question and answer session?

1. _____

2. _____

Type of audience (generalist, specialist, special) _____

Size of audience _____ Male-Female ratio _____

Knowledge of topic _____ Background experience _____

Formal education level _____ Regional background _____

Socioeconomic background _____ Age range _____

Attitude toward your topic _____

Job responsibilities _____

Ethnic background (Are many ethnic groups represented? Are there foreigners?) _____

Personal or work challenges (time management, competition, downsizing) _____

Personal style/image of company or audience (formal and serious vs. casual and laid back) _____

Political affiliations (Who reports to whom? Who's in charge? Who has influence?) _____

Hidden agendas (What possible resistance might you encounter and from whom?) _____

Language (What are the audience members' buzzwords or expressions? Which words, expressions, or jokes should you avoid? Is English their second language?) _____

Special needs (Are there any people who have physical disabilities?) _____

Other _____

_____

_____

tented if you present with an inadequate sound system, poor visibility, or cheap staging.

They're skeptical. Most people today don't trust politicians, city officials, or CEOs. Americans are not impressed by authority and will not accept things on faith. As a speaker, you must gain people's trust and check your information thoroughly for accuracy.

They have information overload. People are so inundated with facts, statistics, data, numbers, and the like that they've reached saturation level. If your speech is a compilation of statistics, you'll probably lose the audience. Provide interesting ideas and help people draw conclusions. Give them simple, practical tips as well.

They're diverse. The workplace has changed dramatically. In the past, management consisted of a white male hierarchy. Today, the fabric of the workforce is multi-ethnic, global, and gender-tolerant. The corporate structure and organizational rules are being challenged. This requires you, as a speaker, to be highly sensitive. You must earn your credibility by understanding today's work culture and issues.

But I Don't Have Time...

Maybe you're thinking by now, "I don't have time to do all of this research for my presentation. My boss gave me 24 hours' notice that I'm going to be speaking."

Not to worry! You don't need weeks to profile your audience. Simply call your contact person and ask a few questions from the Listener Profile. Delegate the assignment to an assistant if you can. You could even fax the sheet to your contact person and ask him or her to fill it in.

Still not convinced? Let's look at a potential worst case scenario. Your boss canceled an hour ago and sent you to present instead. You have a canned presentation you've given over and over. You don't have any information for your Listener Profile.

No problem. Do an on-the-spot analysis of your audience. After you make your opening remarks, poll the audience members. Ask them, "How many of you consider yourselves experienced? intermediate? beginners?" After a show of hands, you'll have an idea of the level of expertise among your audience members.

Look at the audience. You can see the size and the approximate male-to-female ratio. Take people in with your eyes. What do their body language and facial expressions tell you about their interest and attention span?

Now ask the audience, "If you could get only one thing from today's presentation, what would it be?" Poll a handful of volunteers. If the group is small (15 or fewer), you can go around the room and hear from everyone. Now you know the audience's expectations.

Here are some questions I ask in my presentation skills seminars:

- How many of you get nervous when giving a speech?
- How does your nervousness show?
- If you could change anything about your presentation, what

would that be?
- How would you like people to describe you as a presenter?
- Whom do you consider to be a good speaker?
- Have you ever received training in public speaking?

There are two times you can ask these types of questions: before you begin or at intervals during your presentation.

It's best if you start out with only a few questions. If you have lots of questions, make your point quickly after each one and then throw out another. Questions help you gather useful information from the audience while relaxing audience members. The audience appreciates your concern and likes being involved. (Most of us would rather speak than listen.)

So remember: even when you walk in cold, you don't have to be on the hot seat. With some quick analysis of your audience, you can still be confident in providing a presentation you and they will feel good about.

Physical Styles

You'll need to adapt your presentation style to match the style of the audience. Are the audience members loud and expressive or quiet and reserved? If the listeners are reserved and you jump up and down trying to motivate them with dramatic energy, you won't connect with them—they won't be able to relate to your theatrics. Expressive audiences—such as those at sales conventions, women's groups, and advertising companies—will enjoy action, high energy, a faster pace, lots of gestures, demonstrations, and entertainment. They won't respond to a highly detailed presentation with lots of facts.

For quieter, reflective audiences—such as those in scientific communities, financial services groups, and analytical firms—provide theory and detailed information. Slow down your pace and don't dramatize. These people value facts more than entertainment.

What is the physical style of your audience members? There are a couple of ways to find out:

1. **Ask your contact person**. Identify other speakers who were successful with this audience. What kind of physical approach did they take?

2. **Observe**. Is the audience loud, excited, laughing, or smiling? Do people respond with questions? If so, it's probably an expressive group, so you can be more dramatic. If the listeners are quiet, serious-looking, introverted, and taking copious notes, they're probably reserved. Give them facts, information, and detail.

Learning Styles of Your Audience

Once you've gathered information on your audience, you'll have to take into consideration the learning styles of your audience members. Specifically, you must consider two factors:

• Different adults learn differently, and
• Different adults communicate differently.

The more you know about adult learning and communication styles, the more easily you will communicate your message—and the more persuasive you'll be.

There are three basic learning styles. That is, people take in information in three ways: *visually, auditorially,* or *kinesthetically.*

Visual learners see pictures in their minds. They must be able to visualize your message. They're sensitive to colors, and they can describe the scenery from a vacation with great clarity. When they speak, their eyes will look up as if searching for a word or seeing a picture. Their language is another clue to their visual style. Visual learners will use words and phrases such as *imagine, look, get the picture,* or *I see what you're saying.* They will also take notes during presentations. The majority of people are visual learners.

Auditory learners are tuned into sounds. They may hear an internal dialogue in their heads. They often remember conversations they've heard. Many broadcasters and musicians are auditory. When auditory learners speak, their eyes will often look to the side. Auditory learners may also cock their head to one side. They typically use auditory words and phrases, such as *rings a bell, I hear you, listen,* or *sounds good.* Auditory learners need to listen before they can understand. They prefer to listen to a point and then take notes. Better yet, they prefer to tape record presentations and not take notes at all.

Kinesthetic learners are sensitive to touch and feelings. They will remember how it feels to sit in a chair or whether they were comfortable during your presentation. They have to touch and feel to learn. They must do or manipulate to understand. When speaking, they will access their emotions by looking down. Their language makes use of kinesthetic expressions: *gut feeling, get my arms around it, feels good, massage the data.*

There are a couple of ways you can use information on audience members' learning styles. In a one-to-one situation, you can watch a person's eye movements and listen to his or her predicates (verbs, adjectives, and adverbs). Does the person use primarily visual, auditory, or kinesthetic words? Do the person's eyes go up, to the side, or down much of the time? Take the information you've gathered and give it back to the person. If he or she uses visual words and phrases (e.g., "I see what you mean," "Picture this"), begin speaking in visual language yourself. Watch the person's body language and match it. Get in sync. You will develop instant rapport with this listener. Do the same for auditory or kinesthetic types.

But what if you have a large group? That's easy. Always remember to add visual, auditory, and kinesthetic components to every presentation you make. That way, you'll accommodate all three learning styles in the audience. As you're speaking, add visual aids and maybe a little music, then give the audience a short exercise to experience. Let people solve a puzzle in their seats, alone or with a partner. Voilà! That takes care of the visual, auditory, and kinesthetic needs of the audience.

Exercise

Here are various terms that describe the three learning styles:

Visual	Auditory	Kinesthetic
look	listen	feel
imagine	hear	gut
visualize	rings a bell	bang heads
mind's eye	hold your tongue	get in touch with
mental picture	clear as a bell	get a grip
catch a glimpse	earful	massage the data
appears to me	not in tune	skating on thin ice
seems to me	sounds like	feels like

Add your own visual, auditory, and kinesthetic words to this list.

_____   _____   _____

_____   _____   _____

_____   _____   _____

Exercise

What about you? How do you determine your own learning style? One way is to write a letter to a friend. Don't think about what you're doing. Concentrate on the message. Now go back and circle all the adjectives, adverbs, and verbs. You'll start to see a pattern.

I Say Tomato, You Say Tomahto

What would happen if you presented in only one style and the audience members or the individual accessed information differently? You'd have a communication breakdown. Read the scenario below. (Note: It's most dramatic when you read it aloud.)

Moderator: Today we're going to go sailing. You may not be convinced that sailing is a fun activity, so we've asked three members of our panel to describe their experiences with sailing. Let's see.

Mr. Visual: Imagine you're on a shiny, white boat with bright green stripes. As you take off, you see the sun glistening on the water. All you can see for miles is an azure sky with white, pristine clouds. The water sparkles the color of aquamarine, and at dusk there is the most beautiful sunset. The sky is streaked with pink, yellow, and orange light until evening, when the moon shimmers a silvery palette.

Moderator: You paint a pretty picture, Mr. Visual. Is that your viewpoint, Ms. Auditory?

Ms. Auditory: What are you talking about? That doesn't ring a bell! Listen! When I go sailing I can hear the waves splashing against the boat and the sound of seagulls ringing in my ears. You start to resonate with the sea as the wind sings against the sails and you can hear the whir of the speedboats passing by. In the evening quiet, you can hear the softest whispers from across the harbor, and you feel in tune with nature.

Moderator: Sounds wonderful, Ms. Auditory. Does that ring a bell, Mr. Kinesthetic?

Mr. Kinesthetic: She's out of touch! Sailing is a moving experience. You feel at one with the sea as you gently rock to the motion of the waves. You start to relax as the sun beats down on the deck, warming your skin. As you pick up speed, you feel exhilarated by the spray of salt water on your face and the cool, rapid breeze whipping through your hair. As you hoist the sails, you smell the salt air and feel the hard, wet floor beneath your feet. By evening, you're totally in touch with the environment.

Moderator: Thank you, Mr. Kinesthetic. That really grabbed me. I have a handle on what you mean.

This sums up the discussion about sailing. Can you picture yourself sailing? Does sailing sound like a good idea? How does the experience of sailing feel to you?

How do you use this information in your presentations? You can begin or end your remarks by adding visual, auditory, and kinesthetic language. If you're trying to convince the audience to use a weight loss program, you can say, "Imagine how thin you'll look! Can you hear what people will be saying? Feel how great it is to fit into your clothes comfortably."

Remember to add something visual, auditory, and kinesthetic to every presentation so that you capture the interest and meet the needs of everyone in the audience.

Before the Presentation

Just as you don't want to walk in cold without knowing your audience, you also want to understand the logistics of your presentation. It's a good idea to have a checklist to ensure that you have all the information you need to make your speaking engagement a success. If you're giving a department update each month, in the same conference room each time, you won't need as much information down the line. But when you're presenting to a new group in a new venue, you'll need to consider several other variables. Among them:

1. Where will you be speaking? At your company? At a regional office? At a hotel? The location is important. If you're presenting away from home, familiarize yourself with the region if it's in a different part of the country. Check out the weather report and bring appropriate clothing.
2. What is the room setup? Is it a conference room or an auditorium? How big is it? The amount of space you have affects

the tone and formality of your presentation. It can also determine the seating arrangements. If you prefer a certain room
setup, make sure you tell the contact person.

3. What kind of audio-visual equipment is available? If you prefer an overhead projector or a microphone, request it. Find
   out if you'll be speaking from a lectern or podium and, if so,
   what kind it will be. Are you using your Mac laptop when
   the company uses IBM? Check to make sure that the site has
   the correct adapters. Better yet, come prepared with your
   own adapters.

4. How long are you expected to speak? Ten minutes or a full
   day? Knowing the time constraints is absolutely critical. If
   you're speaking for 45 minutes, does that include question-
   and-answer time? A good speaker must begin and end on
   time. If your speaking time is one hour, that means you must
   finish in one hour, not one hour and fifteen minutes.

5. If you're speaking for a full day, how will the day be struc-
   tured? Are you giving several speeches throughout the day to
   several groups? Is it a one-day seminar?

6. If you're delivering a long seminar, when are the break
   times? How long are the breaks?

7. Are there any other speakers on the program? It's helpful to
   know who will precede you and who will follow you in the
   program. This allows you to segue from the last speaker and
   pick up on any points he or she made during the presentation. If possible, meet the other speakers ahead of time so
   that you'll feel more comfortable.

8. What time of day will you speak? Will your hosts be serving
   breakfast, lunch, or dinner? Will the audience be eating as
   you speak? The most difficult times to present are right
   before lunch and right after lunch. Right before lunch, the
   audience is hungry and ready to bolt to get a good seat in the
   dining area. Immediately after lunch, people are feeling
   stuffed—maybe even sleepy. Being aware of your time slot

helps you know how you can energize the group to keep their attention.

9. If the audience members are eating as you present, you will have a greater speaking challenge. Generally, the speaker doesn't begin until dessert and coffee are being served. If this turns out to be your fate, humor is the best measure. Do your best and don't take yourself too seriously.

10. Who will introduce you? Your introduction can make or break you. Ask your contact about this. Prepare and write out a solid introduction. If you have a choice, choose someone you like and trust who is also a good speaker.

11. Is there a fee or honorarium? In some cases, you get paid! Didn't I tell you public speaking would pay off? It doesn't hurt to ask about whether you'll be paid. If your prospective hosts think enough of your expertise to ask you to speak, you can also ask to be paid for it.

If you're going to be successful in delivering a speech, you clearly have to know a lot about your audience, what they're like, and what they might be expecting from you. This chapter has given you a variety of things to consider about your audience and how to use the information you gather to prepare an effective presentation. The following checklist summarizes the ideas I've covered here.

Checklist for Analyzing Your Audience

DO

• **Create a Listener Profile**. Research your audience before you speak. Talk to others who know the group or individuals. Learn about the group's culture, expectations, gender/age mix, education and experience levels, and attitude toward your topic. Determine whether you'll be presenting to a generalist or specialist audience. Learn how particular groups differ.

Don't assume you can speak to teen groups the same way you speak to business audiences.

- **Call the meeting planner or contact person**. The person planning the meeting is an important resource. Ask about the setting for your presentation, the audience, the audiovisual equipment, the time for lunch or breaks, the time of day you'll speak, and how much time you'll have. If you're speaking in another region or country, ask about geography, weather, and behavioral customs.

- **Consider the cultural/political background of your audience**. Since most audiences are multicultural, learn the do's and don'ts related to the backgrounds of your audience members. This will help you connect with them and avoid embarrassing faux pas. If possible, interview some prospective members of the audience before your presentation. Avoid humor and idioms if your audience is foreign-born.

- **Arrive early and greet the audience**. This will reduce your nervousness and help you create rapport with the audience members. You'll also learn something you can refer to during your speech. Even calling out someone's name can go along way toward personalizing your message.

- **Ask questions of the audience.** If you don't have all the information you need, poll the audience. Ask people to identify their expectations. If it's a large group, ask for a show of hands. This on-the-spot analysis will give you a quick reading of the group and show you how to slant your speech.

- **Dress appropriately**. You're judged in part by how you look. Dress for your audience. If you're presenting at a manufacturing plant, don't wear a three-piece suit. If you're speaking at an executive board meeting, dress for success. Be sure the way you're dressed fits the image you want to convey. When in doubt, go for a conservative look.

DON'T

- **Give the same speech to all audiences.** You may give one speech over and over again, but be sure to tailor it to your audience. This means doing some research. Change the examples to fit the industry, the company, or the age group. Add more fun and humor for some audiences and be more serious with others. Add visual, auditory, and kinesthetic components to all of your speeches to satisfy the different learning styles of audience members.
- **Walk in cold**. This is a recipe for disaster. Always know your audience. An otherwise good speech can bomb if it doesn't suit a particular audience.
- **Tell off-color or ethnic jokes.** This is a definite no-no. You'll most likely offend the audience and lose your credibility.

6

Building Your Presentation

If you build it, they will come.
  –from the movie Field of Dreams

You've done your homework. You know the audience and its expectations. You understand the logistics and timing of your presentations. Now it's time to begin preparing, structuring, and organizing your speech.

Remember the movie *Field of Dreams*, when the voice says, "If you build it, they will come"? Well, if you build a well-structured speech, your audience will come to hear you and will stay to listen. Your message is what's important. But if your speech is disjointed, disorganized, or in disarray, the audience won't hear your message. The points you spent so much time developing will simply get lost.

Create a Clear Focus

Structuring your speech isn't difficult. But there are some fairly precise steps you must take.

Begin by having a clear purpose. What is your intended outcome of your presentation? Without a clear purpose or objective, you'll miss your mark—in fact, you won't even know what your mark is!

What is the one objective you want to achieve with your presentation? By answering this question, you will stay focused and give a more organized, cohesive, and persuasive presentation.

Let's consider purpose and focus. Think of your purpose in terms of doing, knowing, reacting, or feeling. You want the audience to *do* something, to *know* something, to *react* to something or to *feel* something. Simply put, you're trying to teach, inform, persuade, or entertain, which we can capture using the acronym TIPE:

- *Teach.* Here the focus is on *skill building*. The audience should be able to do something after your presentation. The key word is *skills*.
- *Inform.* Here the target is *information*. The audience needs to know something after hearing your presentation. The key word is *data*.
- *Persuade.* Here the audience must *change* an *opinion/attitude* or agree to take *action* following your presentation. The key word is *change*.
- *Entertain.* Here the emphasis is on *feeling*. The audience should *feel* good and enjoy themselves during your presentation. The key word is *enjoyment*.

You need to decide if your purpose is to teach or instruct, to provide information or data, to persuade, inspire, and motivate, or to entertain. What if your intent is to achieve all of the above? Congratulations! A presentation that is informative, persuasive, entertaining, and educational (in terms of giving people practical skills) is the ultimate in public speaking.

Your presentation can have all of these elements, but you still need to be clear about your primary purpose. Stay focused. What's the main reason you're speaking on your particular subject? Begin with your written objective: At the end of my presentation, the audience will _____.

Think about your intended outcome. If you're successful with this presentation, what will happen?

You should be able to convey your purpose in a single statement. Here are some good examples:

PURPOSE	FOCUS
To inform	To help people understand the new dress code
To persuade	To convince people to donate money to a charitable fund-raiser
To inform	To teach people the five most common sales objections
To persuade	To get people to buy shares of XYZ stock
To inspire	To get people excited about living in the moment
To teach	To teach people how to drive a car
To entertain	To get people to laugh at failure
To inform	To understand how to create a team
To teach	To demonstrate how to give a speech
To persuade	To help people choose an HMO health plan
To persuade	To convince people to buy an IBM PC
To entertain	To act as master of ceremonies
To inspire	To help people appreciate the simple things in life

PURPOSE	FOCUS
To entertain	To roast the member of the year
To inform	To help people understand the importance of using visual aids
To teach	To teach people how to use word processing software
To entertain	To perform magic tricks
To persuade	To get people to use the Internet
To entertain	To warm the audience up for the next speaker

Exercise

Circle your main purpose for doing an upcoming presentation and then write a clear focus statement for that presentation. Choose one purpose. Do you want the audience to know or do something? Or is your main purpose to entertain?

PURPOSE: Teach   Inform   Persuade   Entertain

FOCUS: To _____

_____

How to Research Material for Your Presentation

After you've defined the purpose of your presentation, you'll need excellent material to make your points. How do you find information? There are several places you can turn to for ideas, material, and resources.

The library and your local bookstore are both excellent places to begin. Get to know your librarian. When you're preparing a speech, a librarian can be your best friend. Here are a few of the many resources you'll find at the library:

• Almanacs,

- Audio tapes,
- Bible,
- Books,
- Church sermons,
- Dictionaries,
- Encyclopedias,
- Government documents,
- Internet web sites,
- Interviews with subject matter experts,
- Newsletters,
- Newspapers,
- Newswire services,
- Periodicals,
- Professional association publications,
- Radio shows,
- Songs,
- Speaker handbooks,
- Speeches,
- Television programs,
- Thesaurus, and
- Trade and professional journals.

Information is indeed all around you. If you know you're going to schedule speaking engagements, start a filing system. Have one file for quotes, another for humor, another for cartoons, another for short stories, and another for statistics. Create files for your topics and place research articles in several folders. A small container of index cards is another alternative for storing information. You can also scan data into your computer and set up electronic files. On the Internet, you can "bookmark" your favorite Web sites and quickly access them whenever you need them. By collecting data on an ongoing basis, you'll increase your expertise and shorten your research time as well.

Speaking Is Not Writing

As you begin writing and organizing your speech, you must realize that the written word is different from spoken language. You must write for the ear, not for the eye.

The spoken word must be recognizable and intelligible the moment it is uttered. The audience won't get a second chance to review what you've said. If people don't get it the first time, they'll miss it. The written word can be reread. Written communication is visual.

As a speaker, you communicate both visually and orally. Your spoken word needs to be specific, concrete, and colorful (vivid). Use the active voice and personal pronouns to cultivate a conversational tone. Eliminate stale phrases such as "It is my pleasure and privilege to speak to you today" or "Thank you for those kind words." Use the word "you" when addressing your audience and the word "I" when speaking for yourself. This will create a personal relationship between you and your listeners. The goal is to talk *with* them, not *at* them.

Structuring Your Presentation

There are three parts to any speech:
1. Tell them what you're going to tell them,
2. Tell them, and
3. Tell them what you just told them.

This translates into an opening, a body, and a closing. No matter what you may think, every effective speech contains these three elements. If it doesn't, you don't have a good speech. It's as simple as that.

Your opening introduces the topic to the audience. In your introduction, you give the audience your agenda or the main points you're going to cover. Why? Because the audience needs a roadmap. A roadmap sets them up to listen and establishes their expectations. If they're guessing what your speech is about, they'll get confused and stop listening. So in part one of your speech, you set the tone, give people the big picture, and offer an overview of the main points you will make in the body of your presentation.

Once people know what to listen for in your speech, you give them the meat. In the body of your presentation, you take each point and elaborate upon it. Go into detail. Develop your ideas. Flesh them out through humor, stories, and examples.

Once you've addressed all of your points, you need to bring your speech to a memorable close. Otherwise, your words will just hang there. So summarize, review your points, and leave people with an action to take. End with a powerful statement so that people leave thinking about your message.

One way to think about this three-step approach is to imagine a "speech sandwich." The top part of the bun is your introduction, the meat is the body of your speech, and the bottom of the bun is your closing. If you examine this sandwich closely, you'll notice that the meat or middle is the thickest part. The top and bottom pieces of bread are equal in size, balancing the sandwich.

To make your speech sandwich appetizing, you need to add

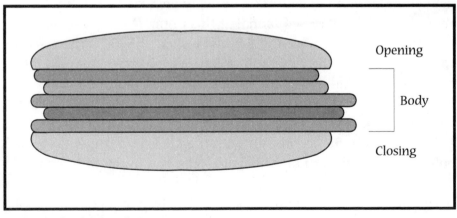

Opening

Body

Closing

A "speech sandwich"

some spices or condiments. Otherwise it will taste bland. So in the meat of your speech, add:
- a few flavorful facts,
- some scintillating statistics,
- appetizing anecdotes,
- mouth-watering metaphors, and
- a pinch of humor.

Delicious! Anybody would want to take a bite. Now, to make your speech sandwich visually appealing, you might add some lettuce and tomato, or a slice of cheese with a pickle on the side. This is the appeal of using visual aids during your presentation. It makes your speech visually attractive.

Now that I've made you hungry, go get yourself a sandwich and come back. We're going to put these principles into practice.

Mapping It Out

One effective way to start organizing your presentation is to use a method called mind mapping. Mind mapping makes use of the creative right brain. According to research on accelerated learning (how we can learn faster and retain more), the right brain processes 1,600 times faster than the left brain does. So this process will help you plan your speech more quickly and easily. Don't worry about being logical or sequential at this point. We're going to use a circular approach, which will break writer's block. (When speakers begin to write out and organize their presentations, they often get stuck if they use the traditional linear outline.)

There are two voices you hear when you're writing: the artist and the police officer. Think of the artist as the creative writer. This is the voice that comes up with the ideas and content. The police officer is the editor. This voice tells you to reword, rewrite, and reorganize.

If you listen to the police officer too early, you'll get stuck. So as you begin writing your speech, silence the police officer and let

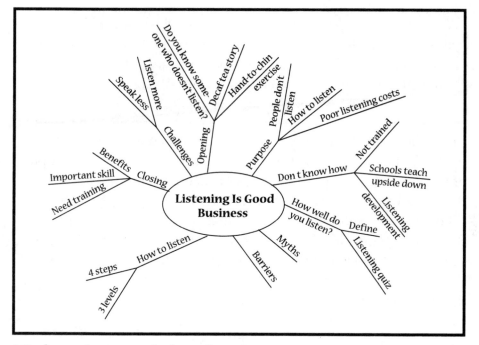

Mind map for a speech about listening

the ideas flow. Don't worry if they're illogical or out of sequence. Don't worry if they don't sound sensational. Just get your main points on paper. Later on you can call upon the police officer to edit.

It's easy to do a mind map. Take a sheet of paper and draw a small oval in the center. Write the title and/or topic of your speech within the oval. Then draw lines radiating out from the oval, one for each of you main points. On each line, write the main point, then create branches from that line for your sub-points. When you've mapped your main points and all the sub-points, number each of the main points to order them in a logical sequence.

At the top of this page is an example of mind mapping a speech about listening. As you can see from the mind map, this speech follows the "tell them" formula. It starts with a question to

Exercise

> Create a mind map for your own speech. Start in the middle with your topic, and draw lines out from it with your main points and ideas. Then start branching out. These are your subpoints and details. Remember: this is not a final outline. You're just putting thoughts down on paper.

the audience ("How many of you know someone who doesn't listen?"). This grabs people's attention and agreement. The next part of the opening is an example of poor listening (decaf tea), which is then followed by an audience exercise in which people stand and follow a quick Simon Says type of instruction. Of course, most of the audience fails because most people don't follow the directions. This interactive exercise creates energy and keeps people's attention. Now the audience members are ready and interested in hearing the next part of the introduction.

I state the three-point agenda:

1. Demonstrate that people don't listen.
2. Show people how to improve their listening skills.
3. Prove that poor listening costs in productivity and relationships.

Notice that in the stand-up "Simon Says" exercise, I've already proven that audience members don't listen. Now I have a captive audience. From here, three benefits are mentioned. Why? Because it's important in any persuasive or informative speech to let the audience know the payoff for hearing you out. If they don't perceive a value, they'll tune out the information.

The next part of the speech is the body. Here I develop the three agenda points and support them with evidence. I begin to explain why people don't listen. They aren't trained! I then define listening and the audience takes a quick listening inventory, which they can score. The inventory once again gets the audience involved and relates the message back to them personally. The closer you can relate your message to the personal experiences of the audience, the more powerful your impact will be.

The message continues to examine the myths and personal barriers to listening. This redefines what listening really is and stresses that it takes hard work to listen well. Next, I prove the cost of not listening and the benefits of developing listening skills.

Now the audience members are ready to hear how they can improve their own listening.

If I had started the speech by describing how people could improve their listening skills, they would not have heard me. They had to be motivated. I needed to change their thinking about what listening is. They also needed to experience firsthand their deficiency in listening.

In the body of your speech, you're building your case, layer by layer. The level of detail you use is determined by the time factor and the audience's tolerance for data.

The last part of your speech is the closing. By recapping the main points, you remind the audience of what's most important to remember. A good recap should offer enough information so that a person just walking in could grasp the main theme and message of your speech. When possible, leave your audience with a challenge. In the case of my presentation on listening, I challenged people to speak less and listen more. They will remember the last thing they heard. Make your parting words powerful!

I love using mind maps, and they often serve as my notes. I can see the entire speech on one page. It keeps me conversational. You don't have to do this yourself. You can use mind mapping to get your ideas on paper and then rewrite your speech using a traditional outline format.

Here's how to create an outline for your presentation.The key word here is *outline*—don't write a word-for-word script. To give an effective speech, you must convert your ideas into an outline that works for you. A good outline has enough information to jog your memory but not so much that you lose your conversational tone. An example of my outline for the listening presentation might illustrate this idea best.

LINEAR OUTLINE

Title: Listening Is Good Business

Introduction: Attention-getting opener.

Do you know someone who doesn't listen?

Tell decaf tea story.

Hand-to-chin stand-up exercise (Simon Says)

Three-point agenda:

- People don't listen
- How to listen
- Poor listening costs: low productivity, poor relationships, impact on profits

Transition: So why don't people listen?

Main point one: People are not trained.

A. Schools teach listening last, if at all.

B. Listening develops before other skills. Cite research.

C. Listening Quotient. Give listening quiz and ask for scores.

  1. Define listening.

  2. Average listener: 25-50 percent proficiency

    a. Myths prevent good listening.

      1. already know how to listen

      2. passive skill

      3. a matter of will power

D. Barriers to listening

  1. assumptions

  2. emotions—list emotional triggers

  3. rehearse answers

  4. judge speaker

Transition: If we aren't trained, how do we become good listeners?

Main point two: Good listening requires skills.

A. Three levels: sporadic, surface, active listening

B. Four steps: attention, comprehension, interpretation, retention

C. Listening CPR: clarify, paraphrase, reflect

Transition: Once you know the skills, what is the payoff for listening well?

Main point three: Listening positively impacts the bottom line.
A. American Airlines saved $40,000 by listening to one suggestion.
B. American Airlines saved enough money to buy a new jet.
C. An insurance company could not settle a $180,000 claim until it listened.
D. Not listening can cost $1 million in lawsuits.

Transition: In closing, we've said that listening is good business.

Closing: Summarize the main points.
A. Listening is an important communication skill.
B. People need to be trained to listen.
C. Good listening benefits the bottom line, increases career success, and improves personal relationships.

Leave them with a challenge or food for thought. And I leave you with this challenge. *Strive to speak less and listen more.* That's all there is to it.

Building support for your assertions. The longer your presentation, the more proof and data you'll add. Once you've researched your topic, all you have to do is to fill in the blanks (as shown on page 150).

Sequencing Your Presentation

Once you've developed your main points, you need to sequence them in a logical order. The mind understands better when thoughts are organized logically. A stream of consciousness approach works on the therapist's couch and in brainstorming sessions, but it's not too effective for public speaking. The audience will quickly become confused.

Title:

Introduction: (attention grabber)

Three-point agenda: (if appropriate)

-
-
-

Transition:

Main point one:

Details: statistics, stories, examples, facts, expert testimony

Transition:

Main point two:

Details: statistics, stories, examples, facts, expert testimony

Transition:

Main point three:

Details: statistics, stories, examples, facts, expert testimony

Transition:

Closing: Summarize the main points.

-
-
-

Leave them with a challenge or food for thought:

You are the tour guide taking them on a journey of ideas, concepts, and data. To get them from point A to point B, you must give them a road map they can follow. Otherwise, listening to you will be like putting the cart before the horse. Your speech won't go anywhere until you organize the ideas into some sequence that makes sense.

How do you decide on that sequence? Here are some helpful hints:

1. **Go from simple to complex.** Start with simple ideas, concepts, and definitions. Add more complexity further along in your presentation. Define terms, give an example, then become more abstract.

2. **Be chronological.** When discussing the history or development of your topic, begin at the beginning and take people through to the end. This is most logical, and it will demonstrate how you got to where you are now. Just be sure to tell audience members what you're doing. You don't want to jump all over the place. Remember the logical sequence: A+B+C+D...=Z.

3. **Go from general to specific.** Begin with a general concept or idea and then give specific examples. Most traditional outlines are based on this model. The main point is general. The subpoints are specific examples. As you branch out and develop your mind map, you become more specific.

Let's Start at the Very Beginning...

One of the most important parts of your speech is the opening. Why? People are terrible listeners. They expect to be entertained. They're overwhelmed with data, and they're sometimes cynical. That's why you must grab your audience's attention from the get-go.

There are several ways you can develop effective openings (not to be confused with a speaker introduction). Most openings fall into one of the following categories:

Startling statement. This could be a statistic or statement that immediately gets people to sit up and focus on the topic. Shock appeal is highly effective in persuading the audience to understand the seriousness of your position. One woman from the American Cancer Society began a speech by saying: "Look at the person on your right. Look at the person on your left. One of you will come down with cancer." She got the audience's attention!

Surprising action. Rob Gilbert, a professional speaker and sports psychologist from New Jersey, has successfully used this opener to grab interest. He slowly approaches the podium, puts on his glasses, pulls out a paper, and begins to read his speech in a slow, halting, stammering manner. Just when you can start to feel tension in the audience, he whips off his glasses, looks up, and bellows, "How much more of this can you take?" He then launches into his dynamic presentation about the importance of connecting with the audience. His technique drives the point home in a memorable and powerful way.

Question. You can start with a rhetorical question that makes the audience think. When posing your question, make sure it's meaningful to the audience. For example, if the topic is public speaking, you may ask, "How many of you get nervous when giving a speech?" For a speech about finding the right job, you could say, "How many of you look forward to Monday mornings?"

Some gutsy speakers will go beyond rhetorical questions to ask a question that begs for a response from the audience. The advantage of this technique is that it gets your audience personally involved and lets you know what they're thinking. Try this technique only if you're an experienced speaker, however. If people respond to your question inappropriately, your speech could backfire—and then you'll have to work hard to recover. It's best to stick with rhetorical questions if you haven't done much public speaking.

Quote. Sometimes a well-known quote can colorfully introduce the point you want to make. This is especially effective in business presentations when you want to acknowledge an industry leader. You'll need to skillfully weave the quote into your topic. For example: "Charles Dickens said, 'It was the best of times and it was the worst of times.' That statement could be made about today's economy. We're living in a time when the rich are experiencing greater wealth; at the same time, the middle class is shrinking. Today we are going to examine Economic Schizophrenia."

Personal experience. This technique builds goodwill and helps you connect with the audience. It helps you relate to your listeners on a personal level. Many comedians take everyday personal experiences and exaggerate them. The audience can relate because they've experienced the same things. Steve Rizzo, the New York comedian and motivational humorist, warms up the audience by talking about growing up Italian in Brooklyn. He tells stories about his father, who was proud to be Italian. Steve exaggerates his father's Brooklyn accent as he ponders what it would be like to have an Italian as president. Almost everyone can relate to stories about one's family life.

Anecdote. A short story is a powerful way to open or close your presentation. The first few minutes of your speech are the most tense. An anecdote or story can help lower your listeners' defenses. People love a good story. It draws them in. But it must lead into your presentation topic or your point will be lost. Here's an anecdote to illustrate the importance of moderation:

There were four golfers who used to go golfing every weekend. One Sunday afternoon, one of the regular golfers didn't show up. The other three golfers saw someone up ahead who was huge and stocky. Thinking they may have found their fourth partner, they approached him. As they got closer, they realized it wasn't a man but a gorilla. But they were desperate so they brought him along. One of the regulars said, "Where is Al?" One of the golfers replied, "He didn't show up so we got this guy.""Hey that's no guy. That's a gorilla!" His partner said, "Look, do you want to play or not?" So the ape took his driver and teed off. The ball went 400 yards up the fairway and stopped one foot from the cup. The other golfers were starting to accept the ape's ability.

Then the ape took out his putter and hit the ball 400 yards again.

Moral: Any strength carried to excess becomes a liability. So it is with communication. If we can't adjust our behavior to changing situations, no matter how positive, it just won't work.

Humor. People love a good laugh. The advantage of beginning with humor (not a joke) is that it relaxes people, makes them feel good, and breaks the ice. When President Kennedy spoke in France, there was much excitement in the press about the glamorous and fashionable First Lady. President Kennedy began his introduction by saying, "I'd like to introduce myself. I'm the man who accompanied Jacqueline Kennedy to Paris." This self-deprecating humor endeared him to the French people and made him seem more approachable and human.

Visual aids. Visual aids can be very effective in focusing attention. In one of my presentations on communication, I begin by projecting a picture of the woman here. I ask the audience what they see. About 50% see an old woman, while the other half see a young woman. This illustration creates quite a stir, especially when people are unable to see both images. It leads nicely into the point of perception and dealing with differences.

Props also make good visual aids. A sales manager once gave a presentation to motivate his sales force. He told them to look under their seats. Taped to the bottom of each chair was a $10 bill. He continued by saying, "It just goes to show you that there's money to be made if you get off your butts." Did he get their attention? You bet!

Purpose statement. This is a direct way of helping your listeners understand your point. This technique is a good choice when there are time constraints or when your audience has a short attention span. For example: "In today's presentation, I'm going to explain the four C's of choosing a diamond." This approach gets right to the point and clearly spells out the nature of the talk.

Begin with the end. Occasionally, you may reverse the order by starting with your conclusion and then building your case, taking the audience from beginning to end. By starting with the end result or bottom line, you capture attention and lead the audience to your way of thinking. Renowned career counselor Barbara Sher used this technique during one of her presentations. She said, "I'm going to start with the bottom line. Isolation is the dream killer." She then launched into her story about how she came to this realization and how it evolved into her present-day success teams.

A human resource manager often used this technique when trying to sell a training program to his internal executives. He would start with the bottom-line cost and write it in big letters across his flip chart. He knew the executives would not sit still until they knew how much they would be spending. He kept their attention because he started with what was most important to them. Once he had their attention, he would explain his recommendation and build a case to justify the cost. He knew his audience.

When choosing an opening, don't rely on the same technique each time. Study your audience and adapt your opening with those people in mind. Reread Chapter 5 on researching and analyzing your audience to remind yourself of the importance of speaking with the audience's needs in mind.

When beginning your presentation, be careful to avoid these mistakes:
- Telling an off-color joke,
- Apologizing or making excuses,
- Letting people know that you gave this speech before, and
- Telling the audience you don't like speaking.

Transitions: Road Signs Along the Way

I can always identify novice speakers. They may have learned to mask their nervousness, but another clue gives them away: their presentations are choppy. That's because they don't include transitions. Transitions are segues that lead the listener from one thought to the next.

Imagine that you're taking a long journey. As you're driving, you don't see signs along the way to tell you where you've been and where you're going. How would that impact your trip? You'd get lost. Even if you did find your way, by the time you arrived you'd be fatigued and frustrated.

The same thing is true for your listeners. You're taking them on a journey, and your transitions act as road signs for your speech. Transitions signal the audience that you're changing gears —you're going to be making a new point or ending your presentation. Transitions create a smooth flow and the fine finishing that adds polish. Another way to look at transitions is to think of your main points as islands. The transition is the bridge that allows you to cross from one body of land to the next.

To develop transitions, think of where you've been and where you're going. For example: "Now that we've covered policies and procedures, let's move on to legal issues." Here are some standard transitional statements you can use:

- "That brings me to my next point, which is..."
- "Now that we've discussed advertising, let's take a look at direct mail..."
- "So far we've covered compensation and benefits. The next agenda item is training..."
- "In addition to cost containment, there is another area I'd like to discuss."
- "Now let's consider..."
- "To begin with, let's take a look at..."
- "The next important factor is..."

- "I'd like to view communication from three aspects."
- "That's the first reason to make this change. Here is another reason."
- "So why should you meditate?"
- "There are three reasons why this is a best-seller."
- "Finally, let's consider..."
- "In conclusion..."
- "To summarize..."
- "I'd like to leave you with this thought."

You can also use physical movement as a transition. By moving from one part of the platform to the another, you give the audience a cue that you're moving to a different point. This is especially effective when you're making a major shift or concluding your presentation.

Now go back to your linear outline and write in each of your transitions.

Developing the Details

It's time to flesh out the body of your presentation. If you simply delineate your main ideas, you'll have a sketchy speech that lacks substance. If you're trying to persuade your audience, you'll fail. People need evidence and support before they'll make a decision. If your intention is to inform the audience members, you'll discover that they won't understand. Listeners need descriptions and explanations to truly comprehend what you're presenting.

In my seminars and classes, one of the assignments is to give a short speech, no longer than six minutes. Every so often, a speaker will finish in three minutes. Since six minutes isn't a long time, why do people conclude so quickly? They haven't supported their ideas. They've constructed the framework of their presentation, but they haven't built the house. This communicates a lack of preparation and a lack of caring.

So let's start building. You can develop your content using a number of tools and strategies:

Facts. A fact is a true statement that you can verify. Facts support your ideas and give your opinions validity. Be sure to check your facts, because today's facts can be tomorrow's fallacies. And something that is a fact to you may not be a fact to your listeners. It's a fact that guns kill. But if you make that statement to the National Rifle Association, the members will dispute your fact. Guns don't kill. People kill. You will lose credibility if you're not accurate.

Statistics. To quote Benjamin Disraeli, "There are three kinds of lies: lies, damned lies, and statistics." Statistics show that the average household has 2.5 children. Not too realistic. Do they have two children or three children? You can see the limitations of using statistics. When used appropriately, however, they work. A startling statistic can have a dramatic effect and wake up a complacent audience. Too many numbers will overwhelm them, however. If you present large numbers, translate them into concrete examples: "How much is $260 billion? If you spent $1 million a month, it would take you 83 years to spend $260 billion." Quote the sources of your statistics—and be sure your listeners respect those sources.

Examples. Examples clarify understanding by moving listeners from the general to the specific. You can use an example of how another organization saved money using the system you propose. You can also use hypothetical examples: "What if your employees were harassing a co-worker? Would you know what to do? Here are some things every manager should know about sexual harassment."

Definitions and descriptions. Definitions and descriptions create pictures in the minds of the listeners so that they can visualize your ideas. If a concept or product is not familiar to your listeners, you must first define it. The dictionary is a good starting place. Further description provides specificity for better understanding. This is especially important in technical presentations. Don't assume your audience knows what you're talking about. Define and describe your ideas before you get to your supporting materials.

Expert testimony. Quoting a respected expert or authority may have more impact than simply stating a fact or statistic. You can use quotes from the Bible, from literature, or from history. Testimonials are crucial for sales presentations, especially if the testimonials come from similar industries. The audience members may be inclined to heed your recommendation when you reference a known authority, such as their CEO, a world leader, or a respected celebrity. When you quote an expert, make sure it's someone your audience regards as an authority.

Case studies. At Harvard Business School, cases are the preferred teaching method. Here's an example of a case study:

> At 3M Company, an employee had developed a type of adhesive. Upon examining it, the company realized that the adhesive didn't stick permanently to paper. Rather than scrapping the product, the company found a new use for it. The product became the Post-it™ note. Do you have a product that failed? Sometimes you have to look at it in a different light. Failures can lead to greater opportunities.

This case study has several applications. It illustrates creativity, innovation, persistence, and overcoming obstacles.

Anecdotes/stories. Anecdotes are brief stories based on personal or borrowed experiences. Stories bring concepts to life by enabling the audience to relive the experience with you. They have great emotional impact and work well when you want to move the people in the audience.

Analogies. These are comparisons that can make abstract material concrete. You can help audience members understand your points by comparing the unfamiliar with something they already know. That's the power of analogies. They're also effective when listeners are resisting your ideas. Analogies often help them see what you're saying in a different light.

Historical background. It may be necessary to provide some background information before the audience can understand your ideas. This is especially true if listeners are new to an organization and don't know the history of the organization, the department, or the product. Take people back in time and quickly move them forward.

It Ain't Over 'til It's Over

Just as your opening is critical for gaining listeners' interest and introducing your topic, your ending must also be memorable. There are several ways to effectively conclude your speech. You can borrow some of the following techniques for closing your presentation.

Tell a story. When you end with a story, be sure it supports the main points of your speech. A story can be a powerful way to end your presentation.

Recite a poem. Use poetry to illustrate and reiterate your message. One speaker I know recites a poem by Ralph Waldo Emerson. Motivational speaker Les Brown ends with a motivational poem that has become his trademark.

Quote someone. You can find quotations in various sources: The Bible, *Bartlett's Quotations*, *Reader's Digest*, recent trade journals, famous speeches, or newspapers. People will remember the last thing they hear. A quotation can have a memorable impact.

Summarize your main points. This is the most common way to end a speech. A good summary should capture your main message. Bring back your three or four major ideas and leave listeners with a challenge. For example: "In conclusion, listening is the most important communication skill. Listening builds teams, improves productivity, and increases the bottom line. As soon as you leave here today, make a commitment to listen to people at home and at work. If you want your life to dramatically change, promise yourself to speak less and listen more."

End with a visual aid. You can summarize and then project your main points on a slide. The slide can remain on the screen for dramatic effect so that the audience continues to receive the visual message.

Bring back the beginning. You can reference your opening and tie it together: "When I began this speech, I talked about the importance of listening in building relationships. As you can see, when people really listen, their lives change for the better. Try the skills of clarifying, paraphrasing, and reflecting feelings. You and your employees will be more productive and more prosperous. Empower someone today. Listen!"

Play music. With multimedia becoming more user-friendly, many presenters are adding music to their presentations. This can be an uplifting method for ending your speech, especially if your intent is to motivate or inspire your listeners. Music is great for team-building sessions and sales meetings where you want to pump up the energy and leave people on a high. Do be careful about copyright laws, however. Don't take any popular song and play it as part of your speech without consulting an attorney or your organization's legal department first. The easiest way to include music in your presentation is to purchase tapes that give you copyright permission.

Your ending is as important as any part of your speech. So when you're concluding, keep the following guidelines in mind:

End on time. It's rude to go over your allotted time. Doing so shows a disregard for listeners' time. It's inconsiderate to the next speaker, it taxes the attention span of the average listener, and it's embarrassing to the person who invited you. If you're running over, cut out some material and get to your summary. Longer is not better.

Keep focused. Your ending should reiterate your main message. Never bring in new information at the end of your presentation. This will confuse your audience. It's especially disastrous in a persuasive talk. You may have convinced people to take action, but once you bring in a new idea you may raise a red flag. So keep your summary brief and on track.

End with purpose. Don't leave people hanging. Sound confident and have a clear, strong ending. Occasionally, a participant in my seminar will end a presentation by saying "that's it" or "that's all." These aren't conclusions. They're like a car that has run out of gas: it stops in the middle of nowhere. Think of marathon runners instead. They know where the finish line is and they move quickly, with conviction, until they break the ribbon. There is a clear, distinct ending. Know where you're going and lead people to a strong conclusion.

Signal the end. One way to let the audience know you're concluding is to tell them. Transition statements such as "in conclusion," "to summarize, "finally," "to bring this to some closure," and "I'd like to end with a story" guide the listeners to the end. They also create a smooth, professional finish.

Checklist for Structuring Your Presentations

DO
- **Start with purpose.** Follow the TIPE formula. Determine if your purpose is to *teach, inform, persuade,* or *entertain*. Do you want people to do something, to know something, to react to something, or to feel something? Be clear about your pur-

pose and you'll achieve your goal.

- **Focus your message.** Be specific about your outcome. Write an objective: At the end of my presentation, the audience will _____. This simple exercise will keep your message focused.

- **Gain listeners' attention.** People are looking for reasons to listen. So begin your presentation with an attention-grabbing opener. Try a startling statement or statistic, a surprising action, a quote, a story, a rhetorical question, a personal experience, a visual aid, or humor. Or, begin with your ending.

- **Write for the ear.** The written word differs from the spoken word. To sound natural and engaging, use concrete, specific, vivid language in the active voice. When referring to yourself, use the pronoun "I."

- **Use mind mapping.** To get your ideas down on paper, try mind mapping. Begin with your topic in the center of a circle and draw lines that branch out. Answer the "5 W's and an H": Who, What, When, Where, Why, and How. Then draw branches from the main branches and add details. This method helps you get started and reduces your writer's block.

- **Outline your main points.** Once you have your ideas on paper, find the three most important points. Then write subpoints to support each main point. Depending on the length of your speech, you can continue to add subpoints and details. This is the body of your speech.

- **Sequence your ideas.** Review your main points and prioritize them. Begin with the general ideas and then get more specific. You can also use a chronological approach, starting with the past and moving toward the future.

- **End with a memorable close.** You can increase the impact of your presentation by ending with something memorable. Try a poignant or humorous story or a poem, summarize your main points, put up an interesting visual aid, or bring back the information you presented in the beginning. Add music to your ending and you'll really have people pumped up.

DON'T

- **Be choppy.** Build transitions into your presentation. Segue from one point to the next to signal that you're changing direction. Tell listeners where you've been and where you're going next. For example: "Now that we've covered operations, let's examine manufacturing."

- **Start with details.** Don't overwhelm the audience with details up front. You'll only confuse people. Instead, build your presentation with a clear beginning, middle, and end. Tell them what you're going to tell them, tell them, and tell them what you told them. The beginning gives the agenda or overview, the middle delivers the details and elaborates on your agenda, and the ending recaps your main points.

- **Skimp on research.** Find information and supporting material in numerous sources. Check out the Internet, trade journals, newspapers, books, audiotapes, dictionaries, and professional association publications. Interview experts or take notice of everyday life. Remember: a good presentation is 90% preparation and 10% delivery.

Listener-Centered Communication: Principles of Persuasion

"One of the best ways to persuade others is with your ears—by listening to them.
–Dean Rusk

So far in this book, we haven't addressed the most important aspect of your message: persuasion, a meeting of the minds. Even if your speech is strictly informative, it still includes an element of persuasion. After all, why should the audience listen to your information? It's your job to convince them that the information you're presenting is important to them.

Most speakers forget this important task. Instead, they simply do a data dump. And some speakers do something even worse: they start their persuasive presentations with their own agenda. They're speaker-centered instead of listener-centered. Even salespeople fall into this trap! They should know better.

People don't care about your product, service, or idea—not initially anyway. They care about their own needs.

Tune into Your Listeners

Most people listen to two "radio stations": WIIFM and MMFIAM-"What's In It For Me? and "Make Me Feel Important About Myself." This is your starting point for being persuasive in your presentation. Begin with your audience.

Common sense, right? Perhaps. But common sense isn't always common practice. Before you can be persuasive, you must study your audience. It doesn't matter if you're presenting to one person or 1,000—the principles are the same. You have to think about what's important to your listeners.

Forget what you want and get inside your listeners' heads. Once you know what motivates them, you're ready for a simple formula that will help you organize your ideas into a persuasive format. It's called HIRBEC, and it stands for *hook, issue, recommendation, benefits, evidence, close*. The HIRBEC formula is the essence of listener-centered communication and persuasion.

Let's explore these six steps more fully. We'll put them into practice later in this chapter.

Six Simple Steps to Sell Listeners on Your Ideas

1. Hook. You have to know how your listeners are wired. Hook them from the beginning by starting with their agenda. What types of things are important to them, generally speaking? What are their hot buttons?

You have to grab people's interest quickly. Otherwise they'll turn you off and tune you out.

2. Issue. What specific issues are your listeners grappling with? What keeps them up at night? What problems or needs do they have?

You must show that you understand the current reality of your listeners and the specific issues and needs that emerge from that reality.

3. Recommendation. Present your idea, product, service, or recommendation. Be specific and clear about defining it, but don't go into a lot of detail. You're only introducing your recommendation at this point.

Lead listeners to a more detailed discussion of your recommendation by showing that you understand their needs, as you did in the "Hook" and "Issue" steps above.

4. Benefits. Remember: your listeners are thinking, "What's in it for me?" So now it's time to present the benefits—to illustrate the value of your recommendation and get listeners excited to learn more about what you have in mind. (Note: Be sure that you present listener benefits and not features of your recommendation or product.)

5. Evidence. Support your recommendation with specific evidence—facts, statistics, analogies, historical data, expert testimony, anecdotes, examples, or case studies.

To be persuasive, you must *prove* your points, not just *make* them. People won't go along with you until you've addressed their concerns.

6. Close. This step has two parts: a summary and an action step. Remind listeners of their issues and how your recommendation will resolve their issues. Then repeat the benefits you outlined earlier. Once you've done this, ask your listeners to take specific action--to make an appointment with you, to give you their signature, to invite you to demonstrate your product, or to simply agree with what you've presented.

People won't take action unless you ask them to.

Listener-centered communication is a simple yet powerful concept. When you approach your audience with their best interests in mind, they will sit up and take notice—and they'll listen to what you say. Most people don't like to be sold, but they do like to buy.

If you're wondering how you can be more persuasive as a speaker, you've probably forgotten what makes people buy: WIIFM! People will buy from you, take action, or change their behavior when they're motivated to do so. What motivates them? It depends, but it's your job is to find out.

People are motivated in one of two ways: they will either move toward pleasure or away from pain. Simply put, do they get excited about future possibilities or rewards? Or do they take action when they know the negative consequences of doing nothing?

The Elements of Persuasion

Once you understand your listeners and know what's important to them, you can present your information from their point of view—and thus increase your chances of persuading them. But successful persuasion goes beyond simply understanding your listeners and giving them what they want. You'll be even more effective in persuading listeners if you also truly believe what you're saying.

Enthusiasm and conviction are prerequisites to persuasion. Let's examine the elements of persuasion and how you can capitalize on them.

Passion. Enthusiasm and conviction are your strongest selling tools. You can have an airtight case, but it won't fly if you have no passion. Would you be excited about an idea if the speaker isn't? Listeners must be able to detect energy in your voice, in your facial expressions, and in your body language. Enthusiasm is contagious. You don't have to pound your fist on the podium. But get excited. Express strong opinions. Vary your voice. Get involved in your message.

Personal stories. Persuasive speakers tell stories. In particular, they speak from their own experience. It's difficult to be persuasive if you position yourself as a third-party spokesperson who is simply reporting data. Persuasive presenters use the word "I," and they aren't afraid to take a stand. Personal stories help you create a bond with your audience. If you're addressing a group of downsized workers and you tell them your story of being laid off, you'll gain instant credibility among them.

Speaking to listeners' needs. This is the essence of listener-centered communication. Until you satisfy listeners' needs, you won't persuade your audience. Psychologist Abraham Maslow provided a map of human motivation with his hierarchy of needs. He said that the most basic needs had to be satisfied first. On the lowest rung is the need for food, shelter, and water. Then come physical safety, a sense of belonging, self-esteem and respect, and, finally, self-actualization.

You can't ask people who are struggling to pay the rent to support the arts. They need to satisfy their survival needs first. People who have satisfied their physiological, safety, belonging, and self-esteem needs aren't looking for more of the same—they're looking for meaning. If you try to motivate them by offering greater material comfort, you'll miss the boat. They have enough stuff already. What they need is balance, peace of mind, and more time for family.

Repetition. Advertisers have always known the power of repetition. Words, sounds, or actions that are repeated are impressed on the brain. People won't remember you very well unless you state your points more than once. You want to get your message imbedded into the mind of the listener. Remember the most important thing in real estate? Location, location, location. You can use this idea by repeating your own word or phrase during your presentation. For example: "What's the most important part of our business? Customers, customers, customers!"

How often should you repeat your ideas? There is magic in the number 3. It's easy to remember things in threes. Many slogans are based on the "rule of three." For example: "Up, up and away." "Ready, set, go." "Tall, dark, and handsome." Benjamin Franklin said, "What I tell you three times is true." Pythagoras, the Greek mathematician, stated that three was the perfect number. We're so comfortable with threes that Winston Churchill's original speech, "Blood, Sweat, Toil, and Tears," is remembered as "Blood, Sweat, and Tears." Milos Forman, when he won his second Academy Award for best director, said it best: "Two feels a little better than one and not as good as three. When you make it once, people wonder if it was an accident. But the second time they think maybe it's not. The third time they're really convinced."

Important things last. Every good salesperson knows that you don't mention price too early. That's a surefire way to lose a sale. Why? You haven't built value. People will find the money if they believe you have something they need. But if you start with the price, people won't be motivated to listen—in fact, they'll screen you out. So state listeners' needs, offer your ideas, and build your case. Save your more important, complex, or controversial ideas for later. You'll have more success by leading your listeners one step at a time and building to a climax.

Savvy sequencing. Julius Caesar said, "Friends, Romans, countrymen, lend me your ears." John Steinbeck titled his novel *Of Mice and Men*, not *Of Men and Mice*. The last element in a sequence is the most important one. You wouldn't say, "for God, for country, and for Harvard." The implication would be that Harvard, being last, is more important than God. The sequence doesn't work. Remember that in a wedding procession, it is the bride who enters last.

Call to action. Many presenters forget how important it is to ask for what they want. You have a reason to speak. You believe in something. But your audience won't take action unless you ask them to. Don't assume that they know what to do. You must tell them. You have to put a demand on the audience. If your association is low on funds, ask for a donation. If it is understaffed, ask for volunteers. If it lacks visibility, ask for media coverage.

What if your audience is your boss? The same principle applies. Don't simply say why you're a good worker. That will only get you a thank you. Ask for a raise or a promotion! It's surprising how few job candidates actually ask the interviewer for the job. They passively answer questions, ask a few of their own, and thank the interviewer. Not too convincing. People remember the last thing they hear. Leave them with a call to action.

Listening. What could be more persuasive than listening well? Speaking to audience needs is a direct result of listening. You need to listen throughout your presentation. By listening to your audience, you'll be able to gauge whether they're with you or not.

Influential speakers listen for resistance and understand how to deflect it. Poor speakers continue giving their prepared speech, regardless of how the audience is reacting. If you suddenly have a hostile audience, address their concerns, calm them down, and continue. Don't be afraid to alter your presentation if it isn't going well.

The Language of Persuasion

Just as there are elements of persuasion, there is also a special language of persuasion that increases your ability to sell your ideas.

That language is the power of the spoken word. Effective verbal techniques include avoiding jargon, using strong words, and replacing non-words with pauses.

Think of the most persuasive communicators you know. They use strong, definitive, and concise language. No wishy-washy language for them! How do they communicate a confident, persuasive message? Why is someone able to take charge while someone else appears tentative? Listen to their language.

What follows are some simple concepts to help you add persuasive power to your words.

Short and simple. Short, simple words have more power than long, polysyllabic words. You may believe that a large vocabulary will impress your listeners. The opposite is true. Long, formal words obscure clarity and distance you from your listeners. Substitute simple words:

Formal	Simple
annually	every year
conduct	run
primary	first
sizeable	large
persists	continues

Just the facts. Excessive detail will bore your listeners. This is especially true if you're speaking to an executive audience. In that type of situation, build strong evidence for your recommendation, but don't dwell on minutiae. Be especially sensitive when giving technical presentations. Give the audience members enough information to understand, but not everything they would need to do your job. Providing too many details only confuses.

Active voice. Choose active verbs to create a sense of movement, energy, and urgency. Job candidates have learned the importance of using active language on résumés. Passive verbs and phrases, such as "responsible for supervision," have no persuasive energy. Change passive language to active verbs, like *supervise, manage,* *direct*, and *coordinate*. Phrases like "just do it," "take charge," and "get going" strengthen your message.

Precision. Vague terminology impairs your communication with the audience. What do you think of when you hear words like "some" or "a lot"? Your audience may know what you mean, but don't bet on it. Managers often wonder why their staffs don't do what they're asked to do. They fail to persuade and lead because they aren't specific in their requests. "We need to improve sales in this department" is a vague sentence. "We must increase sales by 80% in five years" is precise.

When you're putting forth a call to action, be specific. "So I'd like for us to do business" lacks power and conviction. It doesn't tell the listener what action to take. A stronger call to action is, "The next step is to sign the contract by the end of this week." Generalities are weak. To be persuasive, be precise.

Absolutes. Use absolutes to add influence. Words like *always*, *never*, *definitely*, and *absolutely* show conviction. Winston Churchill said in a speech, "Never, never, never, never give up!" Federal Express won an award for the best advertising slogan: "When it absolutely, positively has to be there overnight." Is there any doubt that your overnight package will arrive on time?

Commands. Powerful persuaders use verbal commands such as *must*, *need to*, *have to*, and *give me*. "You must practice these skills daily" is more persuasive than "try to practice these skills." One cautionary note: use commands sparingly. Too many commands will make you sound like a dictator.

Emotional words. These words are most persuasive. You'll see them in print and television ads. They seem to trigger a positive emotional response. The words are *discover, new, improved, love, save, safety, gain, guarantee, money, results, improved*, and *free*. "You'll love the money you save and the results you gain when you try our new product" is a powerfully persuasive sentence.

Another powerful word is *you*. People love the sound of their own name. When you can't use listeners' names, substitute *you*. This puts the focus on your listeners. When they hear the word *you*, they'll be more inclined to listen. Go back over your speech. Circle all the "I" statements. If there are more than three per paragraph, you're too speaker-centered. Reword the sentences to make them listener-centered. By imbedding emotional words into your speech, you'll increase your ability to influence your listeners.

Rhyme. This is a form of repetition that can make your presentation memorable. For example: An apple a day keeps the doctor away. Assonance makes your presentation memorable. Johnnie Cochran, the defense attorney in the O.J. Simpson murder trial, used this technique very successfully. He said about a glove, "If it doesn't fit, you must acquit." This was persuasive on several levels. First, he gave a command—"you must acquit." Second, his phrase had both literal and figurative meanings. It conjured up the vivid, visual image of the gloves that didn't fit Simpson's hands. It also referred to any evidence that didn't make sense or fit logically. Third, the statement gave the jury a strategy for making a decision. Cochran didn't say, "If it doesn't fit, discard the evidence." He said, "If it doesn't fit, you must acquit." Finally, the rhyming became a signature statement. It burned a lasting impression in the minds of the jurors.

Metaphor. The Funk & Wagnalls dictionary defines a metaphor as "a figure of speech in which one object is likened to another by speaking of it as if it were that other." Metaphors make abstract ideas concrete. They paint a vivid picture with a familiar frame of reference. Many business metaphors borrow from war and sports: draw the battle lines, under the gun, Monday morning quarterback, slam dunk, etc. But we're not limited to using war and sports metaphors. Shirley Chisholm, the late congresswoman, compared New York City's diversity not to a "melting pot," in which everyone was supposed to blend into one culture, but to a "fruit salad," in which each piece of fruit maintains its unique flavor and texture while enhancing the rest of the salad. The fruit salad metaphor vividly illustrates Chisholm's idea of maintaining ethnic identity while still being an American. This was a departure from the "melting pot," in which everyone was supposed to blend into one culture. Create your own metaphors to sway people to your way of thinking.

Persuading Listeners by Outlining the Benefits

If listeners aren't getting excited about your ideas, you may be talking *features* instead of *benefits*. Most people don't care about the intricacies of your product or idea. They want to know WIIFM—What's In It For Me? They won't be interested in features until they realize the value of your product or idea.

What's the difference between features and benefits? Features describe the product, service, or idea. Benefits spell out the value of the product, service, or idea to the audience.

You don't buy a shoe simply because it's made of black leather and has a flat heel. You want those features because of what they'll do for you or what they'll give you. The benefits may change with each audience. Maybe someone wants a black shoe because it will match a black tux or a black cocktail dress.

Don't assume what your listeners will see as benefits! You must analyze your audience to determine the true listener benefits.

The HIRBEC Model and Persuasion

Now that you know something about the elements of persuasion, the language of persuasion, and features and benefits, let's apply the HIRBEC model, described earlier in this chapter, to an actual persuasive presentation—one that aims to convince people in career transition to start their own home business.

Exercise

Look at your shoe and begin listing some of its features. Next to each feature, list the corresponding benefit. One easy way to find the benefit is to ask, for each feature, "So what?" The answer to this question is the benefit.

Features	Benefits
1.	1.
2.	2.
3.	3.

Here's a start for you:

Features	Benefits
Leather	Durable. Lets the foot breathe. Quality.
Black	Versatile. Goes with everything.
Flat heel	Comfort.

Objective: To convince audience members to start a home business.

Hook
(What's important to the audience? What will grab their attention?)
Wouldn't it be great if you could control your future and enjoy lifetime employment?

Issue
(What is the current situation of listeners? What are their needs, problems, or challenges?)
Many companies are downsizing. As an employee, you're expected to do more with less, and you find that your career opportunities are limited. This trend is going to continue. What you need is a way to take charge of your career.

Recommendation
(Your recommendation should solve the listeners' problem. Briefly

describe your idea without going into detail.)

The best way to take charge of your career is to start a home business. You can begin part-time and develop it. All you need is a good idea, a room or space in your house, and a passion to succeed.

Benefits
(What's in it for listeners? What will your recommendation do for them?)

There are several benefits to starting a home business. You will:
- Control your destiny,
- Increase your income, and
- Have a flexible schedule built around your lifestyle.

Evidence
(Create a segue or transition to lead into each piece of evidence.)
Transition: Why a home business?
Evidence #1 (facts, statistics, examples, descriptions, expert testimony, case studies, anecdotes, analogies, or historical background)
Fact: Home businesses don't cost a lot and are easy to get started.
Expert: Alvin Toffler, author of *The Third Wave*, states, "The most striking change in the Third Wave Civilization will probably be the shift of work from office back to the home."
Transition: Let's talk about how to get started.
Evidence #2 (facts, statistics, examples, descriptions, expert testimony, case studies, anecdotes, analogies, or historical background)
Descriptions:
- Identify a hobby or skill.
- Develop a business plan.
- Find an accountant and a lawyer.
- Start part-time to test the product or idea.
- Set up an office space with a desk, chair, computer, printer, and telephone.

- Print business cards.
- Let everybody know you're now in business.

Transition: What is the success rate?

Evidence #3 (facts, statistics, examples, descriptions, expert testimony, case studies, anecdotes, analogies, or historical background)

Statistics: According to Link Resources, there are 24.3 million home businesses, with a 95% annual survival rate and an 85% success rate over three years. Non-home businesses have a 20% success rate.

Transition: But aren't you giving up security?

Evidence #4 (facts, statistics, examples, descriptions, expert testimony, case studies, anecdotes, analogies, or historical background)

Fact: Companies discriminate against older applicants. There is no security.

Example: A major corporation offered a buyout to a person who was three years away from retirement. He didn't want to resign so close to retirement. But if he refused the offer, he risked being laid off without a buyout offer in the future. He had no choice but to take the buyout. You can continue to work into your 70s and 80s when you have your own business. You create your own security.

Close

Transition: To bring this presentation to a close, I'd like to recap what we've discussed.

Issue: As companies continue to downsize, your security and career growth are at risk.

Recommendation: You can take control of your future by starting a home business.

Benefits: A home business will provide you with:
- Control over your future,
- Increased income, and
- A flexible schedule built around your lifestyle.

Action: (What do you want listeners to do? By when?) To get started, contact the Small Business Administration for additional information and training. And get started now!

Let's take the Listener-Centered Communication template and use it for your next persuasive presentation. Remember the HIRBEC formula. All you have to do is fill in the blank spaces.

Objective:

Hook: (What's important to your listeners? What will grab their attention?)

Issue: (What is your listeners' current situation? What are their needs, problems, or challenges?)

Recommendation: (Your recommendation should solve the listeners' problem. Briefly describe your idea without going into detail.)

Benefits: (What's in it for listeners? What will your recommendation do for them?)

-
-
-

Evidence:

Evidence #1 (statistics, examples, descriptions, expert testimony, case studies, anecdotes, analogies, or historical background)

Evidence #2 (statistics, examples, descriptions, expert testimony, case studies, anecdotes, analogies, or historical background)

Evidence #3 (statistics, examples, descriptions, expert testimony, case studies, anecdotes, analogies, or historical background)

Evidence #4 (statistics, examples, descriptions, expert testimony, case studies, anecdotes, analogies, or historical background)

Closing

Transition:

> *Recap:* (Bring back the points you made in the opening)
>
> *Issue:*
>
> *Recommendation:*
>
> *Benefits:*
> -
> -
> -
>
> *Action:* (What do you want listeners to do? By when?)

Graduates of my seminars tell me that this persuasive format is the single most valuable tool they learn about. It helps them reduce preparation time, stay focused, and get results. It also makes them much more persuasive in their presentations.

This Listener-Centered Communication template will help you organize your thoughts and focus your message. By writing bullet points, phrases, or a sentence or two, you don't have to memorize your speech. You know the concepts. You can simply make your points conversationally.

Checklist for Persuasive Presentations

DO

- **Analyze your audience.** The No. 1 secret to persuading people is knowing who they are and what they want. Do some profiling and speak to their needs. Don't assume you know what they need.
- **Start with a hook.** Get your listeners' attention by being listener-centered, not speaker-centered. Begin with a benefit statement, not your agenda. Remember the two radio stations: WIIFM (What's In It For Me?) and MMFIAM (Make Me Feel

Important About Myself).

- **Establish a need.** It's difficult to persuade people until you help them understand clearly that they have a need or problem to be solved. If you establish a need, you can then offer your ideas for satisfying that need.
- **Talk benefits, not features.** People are persuaded by what your idea or product will do for them, not by the characteristics of the idea or product. As you describe the idea or product, ask yourself, "So what?" The answer is the benefit.
- **Listen.** You won't be persuasive unless you listen for what people want and need.
- **Save the best for last.** When sequencing your presentation, save your most important points for the end. Discuss your more difficult or controversial ideas later in your presentation. Start the presentation with simpler points or recommendations.
- **Paint a picture.** Use vivid language. People need to visualize what you're proposing. Metaphors, analogies, stories, anecdotes, and repetition will all help you create pictures with language so that you can involve listeners emotionally.
- **Get excited.** Can you imagine a call to action delivered in a monotone? Passion and enthusiasm are contagious. To get people excited about your ideas, find your passion.
- **End with an action step.** Be clear and specific about what you want listeners to do as a result of your presentation. As you wrap up, ask for action and give your listeners a time frame. Without a time frame, there will be no commitment.
- **Prove your point with a variety of evidence, not just statistics.** While statistics can be convincing, relying on numbers alone hurts your case. Listening to one number after another is boring and weakens enthusiasm. Try adding examples, demonstrations, facts, expert testimony, case studies, anecdotes, and analogies. Choose your evidence according to the needs of your audience. Sales and marketing types will respond well to analogies. Financial groups may not.

- **Remember the rule of three.** Three is a magic number. People can remember things in threes. There is a rhythm and familiarity to the number 3. Deliver three benefits, three agenda items, or three main points.

DON'T

- **Use tentative language.** Tentative words like hopefully, might, just, maybe, if, um, ah, and OK can significantly weaken your conviction. Substitute stronger words and use specific, precise language.
- **Look away**. Eye contact is essential to persuading others. Look directly at key people in the audience for three to five seconds. Connect through the eyes. To persuade others, you must build a relationship of trust with them. Trust diminishes when you offer little or no eye contact.
- **Don't promise what you can't deliver.** Better to underpromise and overdeliver. If you convince the audience and then you don't come through on your promises, you'll lose credibility very quickly.
- **Be afraid to take a stand.** In other words, don't wimp out. Be clear about your position or recommendation. Then support your position with strong proof. If you're wishy-washy about your proposal or your convictions, you won't move the audience to action.

Part 4.
Staging the
Presentation

8

Seeing Is Believing: Visual Aids

A picture is worth a thousand words.
–Chinese proverb

Most of us are visual. In fact, studies by 3M, the Wharton School, and the University of Michigan all say the same thing: listener retention increases 70-85% when you use visual aids in your presentation. Visual aids:

- Spark and maintain listener interest,
- Serve as your notes,
- Underscore your points,
- Keep you focused,
- Change how the audience thinks and feels,

- Make you more persuasive,
- Boost your professional image, and
- Help groups reach consensus more quickly.

People will remember 10% of what they read, 20% of what they hear, and 70% of what they see and hear. Do you want your audience to remember your message? Then make it visual!

But before you go slapping up any old overhead or slide, you need to prepare. In this chapter, we'll discuss how to develop visual aids, how to choose the right visual aids, and how to use them effectively.

Let's start with some simple basics for developing visual aids.

Developing Effective Visual Aids

Consider the following tips and strategies in developing visual aids for your presentation:

- **K.I.S.S.**—keep it short and simple. Busy slides or overheads will confuse and overwhelm your audience because people wont know where to focus.
- **K.I.L.L.**—keep it large and legible. The print on your visual aids must be large enough to be seen from the back of the room.
- **Be accurate.** Misspelled words or inaccurate information will hurt your credibility. Proofread your visuals before displaying them.
- **Be horizontal.** Charts can contain more information when you position them horizontally.
- **Be relevant.** Visuals should make sense. If they don't relate to your content, the audience will stare at them and try to figure out the meaning. Good visuals are clearly purposeful.
- **Be colorful.** Color adds drama and interest to your visuals. You can create associations in the minds of the listeners by using color.
- **Use graphics.** The mind thinks in pictures. Graphics are more

interesting than a page full of text.

These principles apply to any kind of visual aid you create. Keep them in mind whether you create your own visuals or have them prepared professionally.

Tips for Using Color, Graphics, and Text

Color

Why use color in your visuals? Color helps you make a greater impact. It adds drama, affects mood, and changes perceptions and motivations.

Here are some tips and strategies for using color effectively in your visuals:

- Include no more than four colors per slide.
- Use dark print on a light background or light print on a dark background.
- Maintain the same background color throughout your presentation.
- Don't use red for text. It's difficult to read.
- Yellow and white print reflect light best. Use them for text, with a dark background.
- Avoid using red/green contrasts. Some people are color-blind.
- Use the earth-to-sky formula when sequencing color—that is, a darker-to-lighter sequence. Start with darker colors on the bottom of your visual and lighten the color as you move up. For example, the earth is dark, the trees are green, the sky is blue, and the sun is yellow. In a bar chart, the bottom would be darkest and would gradually get lighter as the eye moves up.

Color creates associations in the minds of your audience members. So you need to consider your purpose when choosing your background and graphic colors.

Red stimulates emotion. It works well for sales and marketing presentations. Red means passion, desire, competition, danger, stop, error, downturn. Bright red may be too intense for some people. Burgundy is a good alternative. Red is the appropriate color to show a loss: "The company is in the red." Red is a good choice for persuading or moving people to action.

Green inspires involvement or interaction. It's a good color for training sessions or other presentations when you want people to participate. Green also means social, intelligent, open, growth, money, readiness, spring, new beginnings. A green arrow on a slide would signal an upturn or growth.

Gray communicates a lack of commitment or neutrality. A gray background would not be the best color for persuasive presentations. Instead, gray is best used as a bridge between different segments. If your sales module is in red and your marketing segment contains green backgrounds, a gray slide between the two subtopics would work well.

Blue is a calm, conservative color. It suggests trust, stability, loyalty, tradition. Many corporate logos are blue. Where red has a stimulating effect, blue lowers the listener's blood pressure and heart rate. To increase your credibility, use blue.

Yellow is associated with cheerfulness and hope for the future. It also signifies restlessness and change, and it can create feelings of anxiety. Yellow is too bright and stimulating for a background color. It reflects the most light and will produce a glare in the eyes of the audience. It's best to use yellow in headings.

Purple has a mystical quality. It may represent fantasy or take on a childlike quality. Purple is not a good color for business information because it may not be perceived as important. Purple backgrounds are better suited for fun, humorous, or light topics.

Brown is perceived as passive, searching for something solid. So it's best not to use brown for business backgrounds. It will be seen as unstable and less credible than other colors.

Black signifies power and sophistication. Black absorbs all light, making objects appear closer to the eye. A red square on a black background will look larger than it will on a white background. If color can stimulate emotion, black represents the absence of emotion. A black background is ideal for things that have happened or situations in which the audience has no choice but to accept the data. Unchanging financial data or information that is a done deal will work well on a black background. Black removes emotion.

Graphics

How do you choose the right graphics for your presentation? Consider the following possibilities:

- **Bar charts.** These show comparisons or data over specific time periods (e.g., quarterly, yearly).
- **Line charts.** These show data over many time periods so that you can see trends.
- **Pie charts.** These show the relation of parts to the whole (e.g., the percentage of the budget that goes toward office equipment).
- **Organization charts.** These show hierarchy and reporting relationships.
- **Diagrams.** These show an order, a structure, or a flow. Examples: flowcharts and Gantt charts (a chart to visually measure steps and progress on a project).
- **Symbols.** These represent concepts without words (e.g., a dollar sign for money, an upward arrow for growth).
- **Cartoons.** These add humor and interest and get your point across memorably.
- **Photos of a real person or location.** These add realism and personal recognition to your presentation.
- **Graphics combined with bullets are very effective.** Clip art (simple graphics representing different concepts) comes packaged with most presentation software programs. Additional clip art can be purchased separately. Figure 8-1 shows some examples of clip art and how it's often used.

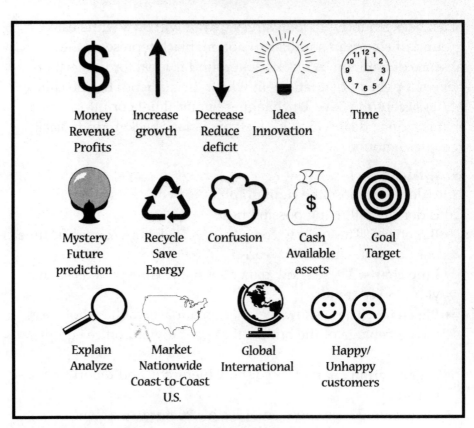

Figure 8-1. Clip art and typical uses in presentations

Text

What's important about text? Consider the following tips:

- **Use short titles.**
- **Create a lot of white space.** Don't crowd the slide or chart. Follow the 6-by-6 rule: No more than six words per line, no more than six lines per slide.
- **Express only one thought per slide.**
- **Use uppercase and lowercase text.** It's easier on the eye and increases retention and comprehension.
- **Use no more than two fonts.** Choose a serif font, such as

Times Roman, for titles and a non-serif font, such as Helvetica, for bulleted points. In the example, the head is in Times Roman, and the bulleted points are in Helvetica.

> ## Public Speaking
> - Prepare
> - Rehearse
> - Succeed

- **Use boldface and underlining to direct people's eyes and to create movement.**
- **Use UPPERCASE letters to emphasize important words in a paragraph.** (Note, however, that if you use uppercase for more than seven consecutive words, your audience members will probably have to reread the visual.)

Choosing the Right Visual Aids

There are several types of visual aids you might use: flip charts, overheads, 35mm slides, videos, handouts, whiteboards, props, computers, and multimedia. How do you choose the right visual aid(s) for your presentation? It depends on several factors:

- **The size of the group.** For groups of 100 or more, you're better off with 35mm slides or computer projection.
- **The room setup.** If you have no table space in your presentation venue, you may not want to use overheads.
- **Your budget.** If your budget is limited, you won't be able to produce a video or rent audio-visual equipment. Props and handouts may be a better choice.
- **The organizational culture.** Organizations often have a preferred medium. If everyone in the organization uses over-

heads, chances are you'll have to as well.

- **The purpose of your presentation**. Are you presenting to train others? If so, you may want to use flip charts. Are you presenting to sell your product to an upscale crowd? Then you'll want state-of-the-art technology.
- **Your comfort level.** Most speakers choose what's comfortable for them. Some presenters may never use overheads because they find them clumsy. Choose what works for you and your audience.

Each medium has pluses and minuses. Let's review some of the pros and cons.

Item	Pros	Cons
Flip Charts	• Easy to use and transport • Interactive • Inexpensive	• Hard to read past 15 feet • Not effective for groups larger than 20
Overheads	• Flexible and easy to create • Widely used in companies	• Awkward to use • Machine can be a barrier • Projector makes noise
35mm Slides	• Professional looking • Show real people and places • No .1 choice of corporations	• Require darkened room • Little group interaction • Create a formal environment • Inflexible
Videos	• Most experiential • Convenient • Free up the speaker • Can be very motivational	• Inflexible and quickly outdated • Very costly to produce

Item	Pros	Cons
Handouts	• Reduce the need for notetaking • Prepare the audience for concepts	• Can distract from the presentation • Speaker can lose control
White-boards	• Interactive • Convenient	• Not professional looking • Require erasing
Props	• Demonstrate something	• Can compete with the presenter for attention
Computers	• State of the art • Interactive • Sophisticated • Instructional	• Expensive • Delay time • Potential for technical difficulties
Multimedia	• High audience interaction • Can combine video and audio • Expensive • State-of-the-art technology	• More difficult to learn • Potential for technical difficulties • Time-consuming

Creating Visual Aids

There are several software packages available to help you create professional-looking visuals. Among the best programs are Harvard Graphics, Aldus Persuasion, Corel Presentations, Microsoft Powerpoint, and BPS Presentation Express. In any of these programs, you can create your own designs or use the templates included.

There are also service bureaus in most cities that will create visuals for you. To find a service bureau near you, look under "Audio-Visual Production Services" in the yellow pages or on the World Wide Web.

If you prefer to use flip charts, there are many books that can teach you how to create colorful, professional-looking charts. See your librarian or the reference person at your local bookstore for ideas on specific books. Or, check out the "Recommended Reading" section at the end of this book.

Tips for Using Visual Aids Effectively

Flip Charts

Flip charts work best with small groups in brainstorming sessions, training sessions, and meetings. Here are some ideas for taking full advantage of them:

- **Use two easels.** You can prepare one flip chart in advance to serve as your notes. You can then use the other flip chart for ongoing interaction with audience members.
- **Start with a blank page.** This will prevent the audience from reading ahead.
- **Place the easel off to the side.** You should be in the center of the presentation. The flip chart is your aid. Don't let it overtake your presentation.
- **Write "cheat notes."** Lightly pencil in notes to yourself in the upper corners of the flip chart. This will help you remember your points.
- **Fold the corners.** Don't lick your fingers to turn the pages of the flip chart. For a more professional image, fold the corners back and then straighten them out. This will create enough air space for you to easily turn the pages.
- **Staple two pages together.** This is another option to folding back the corners. It will make page turning easier.

- **Leave blanks between the pages.** If you don't staple two pages together, leave every other sheet blank. This will prevent the ink on one page from bleeding through to another.
- **Print big.** Use block letters about three inches high. This will ensure that everyone can read the print. Request pads that look like graph paper (also called newsprint) so that you can print straight lines.
- **Pace your writing.** Don't take too long writing on the charts. If you do, you risk losing your audience.

Overheads

Overheads work well for groups larger than 20 but not for huge crowds. To use them effectively:

- **Begin in front of the projector** (between projector and audience). Step to the side of the projector when you're making your opening or closing remarks. This will help you connect with your audience.
- **Test the text.** Place one of your transparencies on the floor and look down at it. If you can easily read the print, the audience will be able to read it on the screen.
- **Use frames or borders.** These will make your slides easier to handle. You can also number the frames and write your transitions on each frame.
- **Practice your writing.** If you plan to write on the transparency, practice using large, legible letters.
- **Bring extra bulbs.** If the bulb blows and you don't have a replacement, there goes your presentation.
- **Don't click the light on and off when changing transparencies.** It's distracting.
- **Put a piece of paper under each transparency.** Many presenters use a hard copy of the transparency and place it in front of the item so they know what's coming.
- **Don't keep talking as you shuffle through your transparencies.**

- **Use silence.** Be silent or use a verbal transition as you change slides.
- **Turn off the projector.** When you're finished with your last transparency, turn the projector off. Don't leave the audience with a blinding light and noisy machine. Your voice should be the last thing people hear, and you should be the last thing they see.
- **Use reveals.** These are strips of paper or clear acetates that create an overlay effect. By using them, you can reveal information a little at a time instead of putting everything up at once.

An alternative to an overhead projector is an Elmo machine. It makes no noise and can project transparencies or hard-copy documents. Just place your paper face up and the machine will project the image on the screen. This allows you to project an original document, such as a company form, without having to convert it to a transparency.

35mm Slides

35mm slides are a must for large audiences. They're inappropriate for small, casual settings. Here are some tips for using them effectively:

- **Number your slides.** That way, if they fall out of the tray, you can easily put them in order.
- **Do the arm test.** Hold a slide at arm's length. If you can read the print, the audience will be able to read it on the screen.
- **Add black slides.** New projectors will go black between slides. But if you're going to be using an older model, create black slides so that people will not be distracted by the previous slide.
- **Bring your own carousel.** This will keep your slides neat and orderly and save you time.
- **Request a remote.**
- **Use movement.** Don't stay glued to the projector. Move into the audience.

- **Gesture.** Move back and gesture toward the screen with your hand. By moving, you burn off nervous energy, look more dynamic, and direct the attention of your audience.
- **Practice with a pointer.** Use a pointer or laser pointer for large screens. But use it sparingly. If you have shaky hands, the pointer will only exaggerate your nervousness. If you'll be using a laser pointer, practice beforehand. You don't want to look like a scene out of *Star Wars*.
- **Use a dimmer.** Don't blacken the room. Your audience will fall asleep.
- **Do a trial run.** Run through the entire slide presentation before you present. It's embarrassing if one of your slides is upside down or jams in the carousel.
- **Don't overdo it.** Too many slides can be monotonous. For a 25-minute presentation, use no more than 20 slides.

Videos

Videos are great for showing real action, demonstrating ideas or products, or motivating audience members. Consider the following tips when using videos:

- **Cue up your videotape beforehand.** Don't waste time waiting for it to start.
- **Check the volume.** Stand in the back of the room to hear how far the sound carries.
- **Pause.** Use the pause button if someone asks a question. This will freeze the action so that the tape will restart quickly.
- **Project the video on monitors** as well as on the screen, for better viewing large convention-style audiences.
- **Make it appropriate to your audience**. Don't show a video with secretaries demonstrating the learning points if your audience is going to be an executive group.
- **Keep it current.** Outdated clothing, music, and expressions will detract from your message.
- **Keep it short.** A video lasting longer than 20 or 25 minutes

will cause viewers' attention to drift.

Handouts

Handouts make good reinforcement material and work well at meetings or for small groups. They're also effective with large audiences as something people can take with them when your presentation is over. You can even create a workbook for training sessions and integrate it into the seminar. Keep the following tips in mind with your presentation handouts:

- **Use lots of white space.** Handouts should be easy to read, with room for audience members to take notes. Software packages often provide handouts with a picture of your slide on one part of the page and a section for audience members to take notes underneath each slide.
- **Highlight your content.** Don't simply duplicate your presentation. If you do that, why do people need to hear you? Use bullet points and verbally fill in the rest. A fill-in-the-blanks approach keeps the audience involved and listening.
- **Place handouts on people's seats or have the coordinator distribute them** as audience members enter the room.
- **Number and highlight your key points.** If you must use handouts during your presentation, it will be easier if everyone is reading from the same page.
- **Pause.** Wait until everyone finds the same place in your handout. Repeat the page number two or three times and don't proceed until people are with you. This keeps you in control and reduces confusion.
- **Check your handouts for accuracy.** Proofread your handouts for grammatical and spelling errors. Use spell check or have a friend proofread for you.
- **Be consistent.** Use the same format for every page. Don't suddenly change the font, headings, or margins. Give the handouts a uniform look.
- **Label all charts and diagrams.**

Whiteboards

Whiteboards are convenient to use in training sessions or meetings. Follow these suggestions to make the most of them:

- **Start with a clean slate.** Arrive early and clean the board. You'll look unprepared if you start your presentation by erasing print from the last meeting.
- **Use appropriate markers.** Some markers will not wash off.
- **Write large and legibly.** To test the visibility of your writing, sit in different chairs and read the print.
- **Be considerate.** Erase any information that may be confidential to your group. And erase the board for the next group.
- **Use whiteboard selectively.** To have the most impact, determine the appropriate times to use a whiteboard. Diagramming or charting a process is a key reason for using a whiteboard. Don't use it continually during your presentation.

Props

Props can stimulate interest because they're tangible. People like to see and feel an object. Remember to do the following when you're using props:

- **Hold the prop in front of you.** Don't obstruct your face with the prop. If you're displaying a magazine or book, hold it still and mention the title and author. Hold it high enough for everyone to see. Put one hand underneath the book with the other hand on the top or side so that you don't obstruct the book's title. If you don't think this is important, turn on QVC or Home Shopping Network. Watch how lovingly they handle their merchandise.
- **Display it attractively.** Diamonds are often presented in deep-blue, velvet boxes to highlight the brilliance of the stone. When appropriate, package your prop for maximum impact.
- **Don't let go of it.** If the prop travels around the room, you will lose listeners' attention. Display the prop in the back of the room or take a short break so that people can look at it

closely. Then resume your presentation.

- **Be creative.** A prop doesn't have to be a product you sell. A magic trick is a prop. It illustrates the point. In a one-to-one dinner presentation, salt and pepper shakers can be props. Sugar packets can be props. It all depends on how you use them. Props make your points concrete.
- **Don't overdo it**. One or two props will do. Too many props will reduce your impact.

Computers

Computers, especially laptops, can be very effective and convenient. You create a presentation on a software program, such as Powerpoint, and then project it for all to see. Everyone should be comfortable with this medium in the near future. Here are some tips for making the most of computers in your presentations:

- **Have a backup.** If your computer crashes, you won't have a presentation—unless you were smart enough ahead of time to create backup overheads or hard copies.
- **Do a trial run.** Boot up the computer before the audience arrives.
- **Request a remote.** You don't want to be stuck at a keyboard.
- **Work the room.** A technical presentation should also be dynamic.
- **Use builds or transitions.** These are graphics or text revealed in stages. You can also use a dissolve or fadeout to move from one frame to the next. This creates a smooth transition.
- **Check compatibility.** Check for software and system compatibility before your presentation. Be sure you have the right adapters and cables. This is especially important if you're using a Macintosh and the company or venue uses IBM compatibles.

Multimedia

Multimedia is a technology that allows you to use several media in your presentation. It combines motion, sound, and text. To use multimedia effectively:

- **Get the right equipment.** To create a multimedia presentation, you'll need a Pentium processor, an additional 500MB of hard disk space, a 16-bit sound card, a video capture board, a dual or quad speed CD-ROM drive, stereo speakers, a microphone, a scanner, a color printer, a VCR, and a monitor. Take time to really learn this medium. Powerpoint, Astound, and Macromedia Director are popular programs that allow you to incorporate multimedia. Powerpoint is the easiest presentation program and the standard in business presentations.

- **Use it prudently.** It's easy to get lost in the technology when you're using multimedia. Don't let it overtake your presentation.

- **When developing the video, consult an expert.** If you've never created your own video, this is not the time to experiment. An unprofessional video will look amateurish when you use it as part of a multimedia presentation.

- **Choose music carefully.** What is the purpose of your presentation? Is it to introduce, motivate, or anchor the topic? These considerations will help you to choose appropriate music.

- **Determine the right kind of overhead projector.** Not all projectors will work with multimedia.

- **Make color adjustments for LCD panels ahead of time.** LCD stands for liquid crystal display projection panel. This device lets you present slides directly from your computer. Dim the lights in front of the room and use a high-intensity overhead projector for best results.

Some Final Thoughts on Visual Aids

Know your purpose. Plan your visual aids. What is the main theme of your presentation? What objective or outcome do you desire? Go back to the original purpose and focus statements you wrote in structuring your talk. Without a clear purpose, your presentation will lack focus and you'll likely prepare too many visuals.

Ask yourself, "Does a particular point lend itself to a slide, or would it be best illustrated through a story?" Write notes on your outline to indicate where and how you'll use a visual aid. Ask yourself, "What kinds of visuals would be appropriate for this audience, this presentation?"

Prepare the last slide first. This technique will keep you on target. What do you want the audience to do? By preparing your conclusion first, you'll stay focused, get to the point, and eliminate extraneous data. In other words, you'll communicate clearly and avoid a data dump.

Eyes on the audience. The No. 1 mistake presenters make when using visual aids is talking to the screen or chart. If your purpose is to make love to your visual aid, I suppose you can continue doing so! But most presenters want a relationship with the audience. That means you have to look at them.

How do you know what's on the chart and still maintain eye contact with your audience? Touch, turn, talk. Touch, turn, talk.

Here's how it works. Touch the screen with your eyes. Get the first bullet point in your head. Pause. Turn and look at someone. Talk. Now touch the screen with your eyes again and get the second bullet point. Turn your head and look at someone else. Talk.

This technique allows you to look at the screen as a prompt. Once you know the point, you deliver it to a person in the audience. Finish your thought before you look back at the screen. Always end your sentences looking at the audience. Don't go back to the screen until you've completed the point.

Check your equipment. Arrive at least an hour early for your presentation. Go to the room and test all the equipment you'll be using. Test your slides and overheads for focus. Stand in the back of the room to check for visibility. Jot down the phone number of the engineer or audio-visual coordinator. Play your video and get familiar with the sound system. You don't want to start searching for the volume dial or the pause button during your speech. When working with a technical assistant, agree on a signal to start the video or advance the slides. Check for extra projector bulbs. Be sure that any long cords are taped down and secure, and that plugs fit the outlets. Ask for extra flip chart pads. Look through the pads and discard used sheets of paper. Assign a person to dim the lights. If you're taping your presentation, do a trial test of the cassette player or video recorder.

Stay in control. Don't let your visual aids overtake your presentation. Gesture, project your voice, and walk over to the screen to emphasize a point. Visuals are there to support your message. *You* are the most important visual aid.

Practice, practice, practice. Your rehearsal should include more than content. Actors have a dress rehearsal before the opening performance. Your dress rehearsal includes using visual aids. Don't wait until the actual presentation and hope everything will work like magic. It takes practice to smoothly transition from one slide to the next. Your job is to make it look effortless. And it is when you practice.

Visual aids can add interest, drama, and professionalism to your presentation. Most important, they increase audience members' retention by 70-85%. Be sure the visuals you choose are appropriate for the audience and venue and that they support your message. If you don't use visuals properly, they can detract from your presentation.

Remember the three P's of using visual aids: Plan your visual aids, prepare the last slide first, and practice.

Checklist for Visual Aids

DO

- **Use visuals when possible.** Most people are visual. They will remember 70-85 percent more when you use visuals aids in your presentation. Visual aids also serve as notes for you and keep you focused.
- **K.I.S.S. and K.I.L.L.** Remember to keep visual aids short, simple, large, and legible. Each visual should be visible to people in the last row and not so busy that it's distracting.
- **Consider color psychology.** Choose background colors carefully. Blue is a good choice. It conveys stability, serenity, trustworthiness. Create contrast with a dark background and yellow or white text.
- **Convert text to graphics.** People think in pictures, not words. Use pie charts, bar graphs, organizational charts, graphic symbols, and photos.
- **Use bullet points.** Use phrases and key words, not sentences. Otherwise the audience will be reading and you'll lose their attention. Make visuals reader-friendly.
- **Practice the 6-by-6 rule.** No more than six words on a line and no more than six lines on a slide. More than that and your visuals will start to look busy.
- **Prepare for disasters.** Arrive early and check all of your equipment. Have a backup plan. For laptop presentations, have overheads in case the computer crashes. Bring the correct wires and attachments, check for the dimmer switch and the switch for the screen, and get the phone number of the engineer.
- **Choose the right media for each audience.** For large audiences, your best choices are computer projection, slides, or videos. For workshops or meetings, flip charts will work, although they're not the most professional. Overheads and handouts are good for small to mid-size groups. Choose your

media by the size and scope of the audience, the setting, the organizational culture, and your personal preference.

DON'T

- **Talk to the screen.** Practice "touch, turn, and talk." Look at the screen, turn your head, and talk out to the audience. Finish your last word while still making eye contact with someone in the audience. Then look back at the screen to get your next point.
- **Use too many visuals**. Overkilling on visuals can be overwhelming. As a rule of thumb, for a 25-minute presentation, use no more than 20 slides. That's less than one per minute.
- **Present slides in total darkness.** Use a dimmer. A darkened room puts people to sleep. Have enough light so that there is good resolution on the screen and the audience can see your face.
- **Distribute handouts during your presentation.** Wait until after the speech. Otherwise, your audience will thumb through the pages of the handouts and won't pay attention to you.
- **Use red for text.** Red tires the eyes. Use red only for underlining or graphics. Red doesn't reflect light well, and red print will appear muddy.

9

Setting
the Stage

All the world's a stage.
–William Shakespeare

*I*t's time to stage your presentation. This is a fairly easy task, once you know what to do.

In this chapter, we'll discuss how you can select the right room setup for your presentation, how to work with lecterns and microphones, how to use notes, and how to create a positive environment that's conducive to the purposes of your presentation.

Room Setup

In some cases, you'll have absolutely no choice in how the room is arranged. But when you can take charge, do so. The arrangement of the room can have a positive or negative effect on your presentation.

How do you plan to set up the room? It starts with your purpose. Ask yourself these questions:

1. What kind of presentation am I giving?
   - keynote
   - meeting or seminar
   - workshop
   - sales call
   - team presentation
2. How large is my audience?
   - 10 or fewer
   - 10-25
   - 25-100
   - over 100
   - 1,000-plus
3. How formal is the group?
   - casual, relaxed
   - relaxed but business-like
   - formal
4. How large is the room?
   - small meeting room
   - classroom size
   - banquet room
   - auditorium
   - stadium
5. How much audience interaction will there be?
   - none
   - only a question-and-answer period
   - some audience exercises

- ongoing interaction
6. How long will I speak?
   - ten minutes
   - one hour
   - two hours
   - half a day
   - full day
   - several days

Once you know the answers to these questions, you can make intelligent choices about arranging the room. If you're speaking at a conference or convention, the meeting planner or banquet coordinator will help you decide. Either will often have diagrams of the room and will tell you what room setup is realistic. Call in advance to discuss your requirements. Don't wait until the morning of your presentation and expect that the room setup will be to your liking. You must ask for what you want.

Room Setup Options

When you're thinking about the setup of your presentation room, there are many options to consider. Let's look at the different room setups at your disposal:

Theater style. This is the most common room setup for large groups. It's the one used in most auditoriums. If you know you'll be speaking in an auditorium or theater, you probably have no setup option. The seats are bolted to the floor in rows. The stage platform is up front. The advantage of theater style is that it can accommodate large numbers of people. It's also the most traditional and formal configuration. The disadvantage of this setup is that the speaker is separated from the audience. It's more difficult (but not impossible) to create intimacy with your listeners.

Conference style. This room arrangement is very common for company meetings. People sit around a large boardroom table

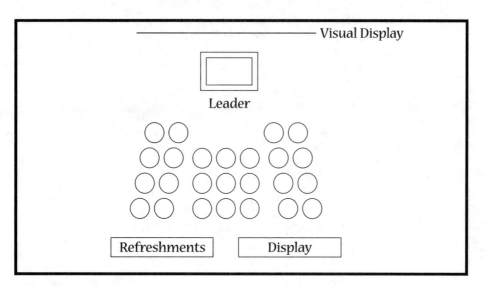

Theater-style setup

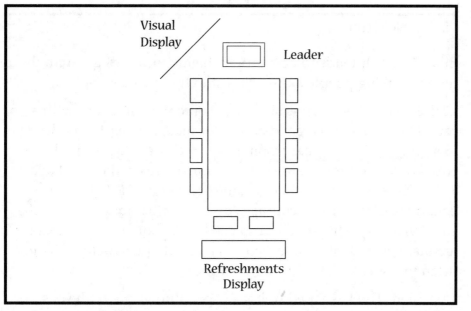

Conference-style setup

with the speaker seated or standing at the front of the table. This
works best for groups of 12 to 15 and when the purpose is to relay

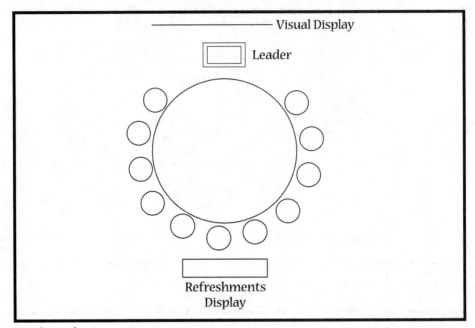

Circle style-setup

information. It tends to be a formal, hierarchical design, with the higher-ranking people sitting closest to the speaker.

Circle style. This setup is similar to conference style but with a round table. It's also a good choice for meetings, and it tends to be less formal than the boardroom table. Because it lacks the sharp edges of the conference table, there is no clear head of the table. This creates a more democratic atmosphere in which everyone's equal. The circle also encourages discussion because everyone has equal visibility. This style is also used for banquets where there are many round tables and people can easily turn their chairs to listen to a speaker after eating their meal.

U-shaped. The U-shaped or horseshoe setup is one of the best for training and classroom learning. Like the circle, it encourages discussion. It also creates an open path for the speaker to walk in and out of the group. By working the room this way, you can create an intimacy that fosters open discussion. This is an excellent setup for team building and management training.

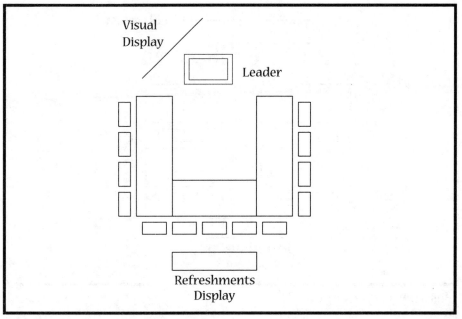

U-shaped or horseshoe-style setup

Classroom style. The classroom setup is the most common arrangement for seminars. It consists of tables and chairs set up in rows. This arrangement is more practical than theater style because participants will be expected to write during the session. It tends to be more formal than U-shaped, but it accommodates more people.

Chevron style. This setup is a variation of classroom style. The tables and chairs are angled rather than in straight rows. This angling can improve visibility for your audience.

Team style. When you require a high level of interaction from the group, team style may be your best choice for room setup. In this setup, tables and chairs are in separate groups, each with its own flip chart and other materials that might be needed. Whenever there's a team exercise, the groups are already in their teams. This is a great timesaver as well as a way to bond with audience mem-

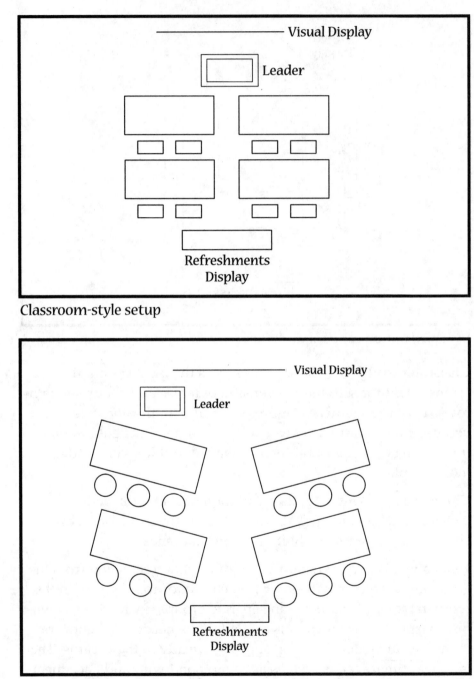

Classroom-style setup

Chevron-style setup

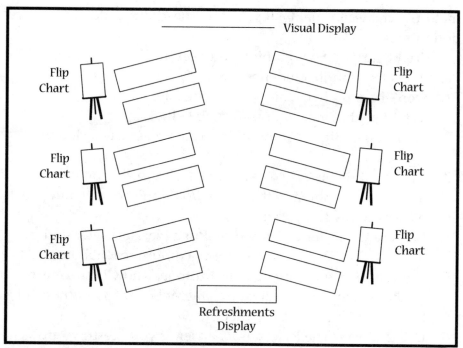

Team-style setup

bers. This pattern is ideal for team-building sessions, facilitating groups, diversity training, and creative problem solving.

Lecterns and Microphones

You've chosen the best room setup for your presentation, so you're ready to roll, right? Not yet. What about your equipment? We haven't talked about lecterns and microphones.

Using the Lectern

First of all, do you really need a lectern? I know what you're thinking—you can use the lectern to hide behind! But there's only one good reason for using a lectern—to hold your notes.

A lectern is a barrier between you and your audience. It automatically creates formality. If you don't need it to hold your notes, don't use it.

Alright, alright. So you think you need it. How do you use it? Here are a few simple guidelines:

1. **Don't lean on it.** Create some space. Step back from the lectern so that you can't lean against it.
2. **Stand up straight.** Slumping posture will create a sloppy appearance.
3. **Anchor your feet.** If you sway back and forth, you'll look like a buoy bobbing in the water. You don't want to put people to sleep with hypnotic movement.
4. **Prepare the lectern in advance**. Put a glass of water underneath it. Position your notes for maximum readability.
5. **Get familiar with any dials or buttons.** Know how to turn on the reading light. Adjust the microphone. You don't want to be fumbling with the panel.
6. **Use gestures.** The lectern is a barrier. If your gestures are waist high, your audience members won't see them. If you don't use gestures, you'll appear stiff.
7. **Push your energy.** You're not entirely visible and you're reading your notes. So increase your vocal variety and enthusiasm. It may seem exaggerated to you, but it will sound just right to the audience.
8. **Step to the side of the lectern.** Don't stay glued behind a wall of wood. Begin your presentation by stepping out in front to make your opening remarks. Then step behind the lectern to begin your speech. Find places where you can come out once again by telling a short story or giving an example. This helps you to connect with the audience.
9. **Adjust the lectern for height.** In some cases, you may be able to request a special lectern if you're very tall or very short. If you're shorter than 5 feet 2 inches, you may want to stand on a platform behind the podium to give you added height. Another option is to use a table podium.

Managing the Microphone

Whether or not you choose to use a lectern, you may need a microphone if you're addressing a group of fifty or more. Trained orators may be able to project their voices to the back row of an amphitheater without amplification, but the average presenter will need to use some kind of microphone.

What should you know about using a microphone? The first point is to know what type of microphone you'll be using. There are several options.

Attached. Many lecterns have a microphone built in. This is the least desirable model because it requires you to stay glued behind the lectern. When you're using an attached mike, position it so it's close enough to your mouth to pick up sound but not so close that you're swallowing it. You shouldn't have to lean in to talk. Keep your head up and speak directly to the crowd. And be careful not to turn your head. One speaker I know turned her head each time she projected a new slide. When she turned to look at the screen, people in the audience couldn't hear what she was saying.

Lavaliere. A lavaliere microphone goes around your neck. It frees you to concentrate on your message and not on the microphone. The lavaliere also allows you to move away from the lectern. Just be sure to request a long enough cord, and be careful not to trip on it when you walk.

Handheld. Some presenters prefer a handheld microphone. It gives them something to do with their hands. You'll need to practice holding this kind of microphone the right distance from your mouth. If it's too close, you'll get extra plosion when pronouncing "p" and "b" words. If it's too far away, it won't pick up your voice. Check to see that the switch is turned on. There's one occasion when you'll definitely want a handheld mike: when you plan to have audience interaction, you'll need this kind of microphone to pick up questions and comments from the audience.

Cordless. This is the microphone of choice. It's compact, it clips onto your lapel, and the battery pack is placed in your back pocket or clipped to your waist. It's lightweight so that you can forget about it, and you don't have to worry about tripping over cords. One cautionary note to female presenters: Wear a suit with a jacket. There will be no place to attach the battery pack to a dress. And a jacket will hide it from the audience if you should suddenly pivot. One other word of caution: if you're going to take a break, be ever vigilant about turning off the mike. One woman forgot to turn hers off when she went to the rest room. Talk about embarrassing moments!

There are a few points to keep in mind about using a microphone:

- Let the meeting planner know what kind of microphone you want to use.
- Arrive early and practice with the equipment. Know how to turn the microphone on and off and adjust the volume.
- Don't yell. You can speak in a normal tone. The microphone will amplify your voice.
- If your audience seems to be straining to hear you, ask them if you're speaking loudly enough.
- Have a backup plan. Ask for an additional microphone. During the 1996 Republican Convention, Elizabeth Dole requested two mikes. When the first one failed, her assistant was right there with a backup.
- If you're taping your presentation, be sure to have a handheld mike to pick up audience questions and comments.

Visual Aids, Pictograms, Notecards, and Manuscripts

Notes can be a help or a hindrance, depending on how you use them. There are four forms of notes available: visual aids (slides or overheads), pictograms, notecards, and manuscripts.

Visual aids. Using visual aids as your notes creates a polished, professional image. You sound more confident when you don't have to read your notes word for word. The bullets in your visual aids serve as an outline or agenda, giving you ample opportunity to deliver your own stories and examples. The visuals also enhance the attention, comprehension, and retention of the audience members.

Pictograms. A pictogram, or picture script, works well when you're delivering a slide presentation. Take an 8 1/2-inch by 11-inch piece of paper and create six to eight boxes on it. Draw a picture, symbol, or graphic to illustrate the points you're making. Instead of reading words, you're seeing pictures and delivering these concepts to your listeners.

The advantage of the picture script is that it prevents you from reading, allows you to sound conversational, and helps you have more eye contact with the audience. Your listeners don't see the picture. It's your job to create images and concepts for them.

A variation of the pictogram is to add some text. Draw a visual on the lefthand side of the paper. On the righthand side, write two or three words or bullet points. Keep it brief; otherwise you'll be tempted to read. Don't write full sentences or paragraphs.

When you're using a pictogram, be sure to number your pages as well as each visual box. That way, you'll be able to put the pages together again quickly if you drop them.

Keep the visuals in your pictogram simple. You can draw them by hand or use one of the numerous clip art programs to find the best graphics. Don't overwhelm your eyes. Keep graphics clean and crisp. (Note: Powerpoint software has a built-in pictogram feature. It allow you to see a reduced version of the visual and includes space for writing notes.)

Notecards. Many speakers feel comfortable writing notes on

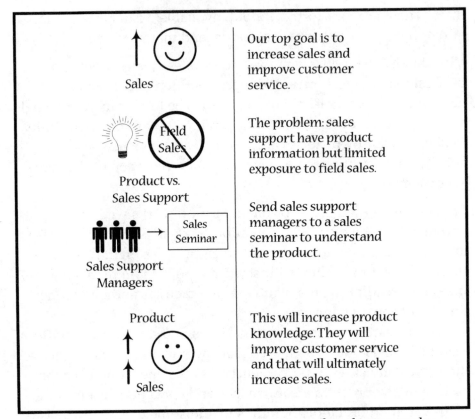

Our top goal is to increase sales and improve customer service.

The problem: sales support have product information but limited exposure to field sales.

Send sales support managers to a sales seminar to understand the product.

This will increase product knowledge. They will improve customer service and that will ultimately increase sales.

Example of pictogram with the meaning translated into words

index cards. If you choose this method, opt for 5-inch by 7-inch cards. Type or print legibly using large block letters. It's embarrassing when you step up to the lectern and you can't read your notes. Underline key words to add emphasis in your delivery, but don't write a word-for-word script. Remember: this is an outline. Use key words and phrases. Just as with the pictogram, number your notecards and practice with them out loud.

If you don't have a lectern and you must hold the cards in your hands, here's a tip for making them less obtrusive. Use sheets of 8 1/2-inch by 11-inch paper and staple them to pieces of colored construction paper to match your attire. If you're wearing navy blue, navy blue construction paper will blend in with your clothes, giving you a more finished look than holding white cards.

Manuscripts. Avoid this method if you can, because it's the most difficult to master. There are certain situations, however, when a manuscript is the best choice. If you're going to represent a company or industry, the legal department may want to go through your speech with a fine-tooth comb. Or perhaps your speech is going to be reprinted in the media—if so, a word-for-word script will be necessary.

The misconception about manuscripts is this: speakers think it's easier to have every word written down for them. But in actuality, a manuscript simply serves as a crutch, one that can turn into a self-defeating club if you're not an experienced presenter. Here are some disadvantages of using a manuscript for your presentation:

- **You can lose your place.** If this happens, there's nothing you can do but endure embarrassing silence until you scan the document to get back on track.
- **You sound canned.** It's difficult to sound conversational and energetic when you're reading a manuscript. Ronald Reagan was a master at speaking from a manuscript. Most of us aren't.
- **You sacrifice eye contact with your audience.** Ronald Reagan had a teleprompter. It takes practice to read and maintain eye contact with your audience. Without strong, ongoing eye contact, you don't connect with your listeners.

So how do you make the manuscript work for you?

1. **Organize carefully.** Build an outline first. One thought must build upon another. Build in transitions to signal when you're making a new point. Number each page in the upper righthand corner.
2. **Make it reader-friendly.** Begin by framing each page with lots of white space. Allow top and bottom margins of at least a half inch and side margins of an inch or more to allow for writing notes and reminders. Use a large font—14-point or

18-point—and triple space. Use uppercase and lowercase letters. All caps is more taxing to your eye.

3. **Keep it loose.** Don't staple the pages of your manuscript. This will cause you to flip the pages. Instead, place the first page on the lefthand side and the rest of the pile on the right. As you finish page one, slide page two from the right pile to the lefthand side. Sliding is more professional than noisily flipping pages.

4. **Mark it up.** Marking up your manuscript must be part of your preparation. You may have rehearsed with confidence, but in the pressure of the moment you can forget to pause, emphasize the wrong word, or lose your place.

   Start by putting in slashes to remind yourself to pause. A single slash (/) indicates a short pause. A single slash breaks a sentence into manageable bits, much like a comma. Hold this pause for about one-and-a-half seconds. A double slash (//) represents a long or dramatic pause. Place a double slash at the end of a sentence or when you want to create emotional impact. Pause for about two-and-a-half seconds for a double slash. Underline key words with a red pen or yellow highlighter. These are the important buzzwords, hot buttons, or emotion words, like "success," "value," "market

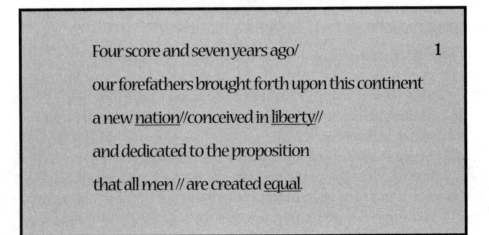

share," and "vision." By underlining key words, you'll remind yourself to project your voice with passion and conviction.

5. **Make margin notes**. In the margins of your manuscript, write reminders to smile, slow down, gesture, or tell a story. Since you'll know your story well, you don't have to write it out. Make a note in the margin to tell your anecdote or story and draw an arrow to the section where it fits in.

   At that point, step away from the lectern and talk to the audience. Tell your story from the heart. Connect with the audience. When you finish your story, step back to the lectern. The arrow in your notes will indicate where you are in the script so that you can smoothly pick up where you left off. By building in these short anecdotes and stories, you'll connect better with the audience and be more professional.

6. **Use strong eye contact**. This is extremely challenging if you're using a manuscript. How do you read and make eye contact with the audience? Here's the key. Pick up the first phrase or sentence in your mind. Look out at the audience and speak it. Finish the last word by looking at someone. When you've spoken your last word, pause. Bring your eye contact back to the next phrase or sentence. Speak it out. Come back and do it again. Always finish the sentence looking out at someone, and remember to pause.

7. **Rehearse**. As you can probably see, it's going to take some practice to get the hang of speaking from a manuscript. So run through the script a few times until you're comfortable with it. Practice pauses and eye contact. Rehearse walking away from the lectern to tell your story. Keep in mind that a rehearsal will run shorter than the actual presentation. So if it takes 20 minutes to rehearse, the actual presentation will run about 30 minutes.

Creating a Positive Atmosphere

Once you've set up the room, tested the microphone, and practiced with notes behind a lectern, how do you keep your audience
with you? By creating a comfortable environment.

Imagine people starting to squirm in their seats. Some are fan-
ning themselves. Others are adjusting their jackets. Some people
are nodding off. When this happens, your audience has stopped
listening and learning.

It's your job (and the meeting planner's job) to create a positive atmosphere for the audience. You begin by satisfying physical
needs.

When you arrive for your speaking engagement, check the
room. How is the temperature? Even if it's temperate, get the
engineer's phone number. Have him or her show you how to
work the thermostat. It may be comfortable now, but once the
room fills up the audience's body heat will raise the temperature.
It's better to have the room slightly cool so that people will stay
alert.

Next, check the lighting. If there will be a spotlight on you,
rehearse with that type of lighting. Locate the dimmer switch so
that you don't have to put the audience in total darkness when
you're projecting slides. Better yet, assign someone to hit the
switch.

If your audience will be arriving first thing in the morning,
provide food. Coffee and some fresh muffins or bagels go a long
way toward setting a positive tone. People bond around food, and
it's a great social icebreaker.

For a seminar, provide lunch or give participants an hour to
eat. As lunchtime approaches, people get hungry and stop listening. Keep your content light and don't hold people longer than
necessary. If you're ordering in for lunch, make sure there's something everyone will eat. More and more people are vegetarians
and/or health conscious. Vegetables, tuna, cold cuts, and light sal-

ads work best.

Most important, remember the afternoon slump. Have cookies and sodas for that quick sugar high. Energy starts to plummet in the afternoon, so the audience may need more frequent breaks.

For evening presentations, provide cheese, fruit, and crackers. At the very least provide some coffee and tea or pitchers of water. Many people will be coming straight from work and will want something to nosh on.

Once people's physical needs are satisfied, you'll want to consider their social needs. Greet people with a smile and let them know you're happy to meet them. One speaker, Andrea Nierenberg, president of the Nierenberg Group, stands at the door and shakes hands with every person who enters. By the time she's on stage, she already has a rapport with the audience.

While you're chatting with one person, you can facilitate introductions to other audience members. There will be some people who don't know anyone, and they'll appreciate your hospitality.

Try beginning your presentation with a group icebreaker. For small groups, individual introductions can work. Otherwise, get people standing or talking to the person next to them. This creates energy and a sense of fun and involvement.

If you're giving a longer presentation or seminar, there are other considerations for creating a positive atmosphere that promotes learning. For example, you can waste a lot of time if you're not organized, and this can put members of the audience into a negative frame of mind. Here are some common time killers and time savers to be aware of and to use:

Time Killers	Time Savers
Start late.	Start on time, even if you have only half of the class.
Distribute handouts one by one.	Put a packet on each seat beforehand.
Allow discussions to linger.	Summarize and move on.

Time Killers	Time Savers
Write out each point as you go.	Prepare flip charts and visuals in advance.
Wait for people to volunteer.	Call on people.
	Get volunteers at break.
Spend too long dealing with resistant participants.	Offer to speak with them privately.
Try to get information from a fatigued group.	Give people a short break.
	Stimulate thinking by charting a list of ideas from which they can choose.
Have every small group report back to the whole.	Each group reports only one item. Write the most important points on a flip chart and post them on a wall.

The First Thirty Minutes

You can lose your audience if you don't set a positive tone from the start and meet the needs of the individual listeners. Some people are impatient to get started. Others think they're experts and that they don't need the information you'll be presenting. Some will dislike your style, and some will have concerns about confidentiality. A few will even be conflicted about their jobs and personal problems.

With some or all of these things potentially going on, what's a presenter to do to create a good atmosphere and set the stage for success? Here are a few tips:

- **Start on time**. Emphasize the objectives of your presentation. Mention the benefits. Remember WIIFM—What's in it for me?
- **Assess the different levels of competence among the audience members.** Acknowledge the experts in the room. Act as a

facilitator rather than the chief expert. Address the concerns of the experts and the novices. Explain how experts can share valuable experiences and how novices can offer a fresh perspective.

- **Create an adult-to-adult atmosphere to neutralize your perceived superiority.** Establish an interaction, not a student-teacher relationship. Ask for listeners' ideas. This will minimize resistance and give you credibility.
- **Mention that confidentiality will be respected.** If you'll be discussing some sensitive issues, people may be reluctant to participate. Tell listeners that you'll focus on common themes but not individual comments.
- **Review your agenda and ask for feedback.** Ask, "Does this meet your expectations?" and "Is there anything else we should cover?" Asking these questions at the start will eliminate unfulfilled expectations later.

The BASH Approach to Setting the Stage

When you're presenting a seminar or training session, get off to a good start by remembering the BASH formula: **b**reaks, **a**ttitude, **s**et the stage, and **h**ousekeeping.

Breaks. People need short, frequent breaks to stay alert and focused. Aim for a short break after every hour of instruction if possible. Then resume your presentation on time. Don't wait for latecomers or you'll lose valuable time. Be sensitive to special situations as well. You may have to provide longer breaks to allow participants to take care of office business.

Attitude. Be positive, supportive, and flexible. When challenged, remain calm and non-defensive. Be willing to depart from your agenda if it isn't working. Ask the audience members how they're reacting to your presentation, and be sensitive to nonverbal signals. Support the learners' self-esteem, and they will take risks.

Set the stage. First impressions can have a strong effect on the success of your presentation. So start on a positive note! Keep your energy high and begin on time. This is the time to create excitement. Let people know what they'll learn and why. Establish your credibility by giving your background and explaining your role in the learning process. (See "Positioning Your Presentation" below.) Present the agenda so that listeners know what to expect.

Housekeeping. Take care of "housekeeping" items early on. Establish the amount of time for breaks, the location of the restrooms, your start and finish times, lunch arrangements, the need for notetaking, and any other important housekeeping details.

Positioning Your Presentation

As you can see, setting the stage for your presentation involves more than bells and whistles. Behind-the-scenes preparation is critical to your success—as is positioning your presentation.

Every audience is thinking three things:

1. **Who are you?** Who are you as a person? Are you friend or foe? Can I trust you?
   Solution: Establish rapport. Tell them something personal about yourself.
2. **Who are you to tell me?** What are your credentials? What gives you the right to speak about this topic?
   Solution: Tell them about your professional background
3. **What's in it for me?** Why should I listen to you? What will I get out of it?
   Solution: Give them the benefits to their jobs, their lives. Tailor this for each audience.

How do you position your presentation? Try the BAER formula: **b**ackground, **a**genda, **e**xpectations, and **r**oles. Let's look at an example.

Background

"Good morning. Welcome to the Train-the-Trainer seminar. I'm Susie Speaker and I will be your seminar leader. I live in Grand Rapids, Michigan, with my husband Jim, my 7-year-old daughter, Kaitlin, and my terrier, Skippy. This is my first trip to Memphis and I was so excited to see Graceland. It's good to be here.

"My company is Speak Right, and I've been in the training industry for more than fifteen years. This program has been delivered to companies such as AT&T, Met Life Insurance, Merck, and Disney.

"What we find is that more managers and subject matter experts are taking on the responsibility for training others. This four-day program is designed to give you the tools and techniques for enhancing your presentation skills and delivering more effective training sessions."

Agenda

"The format is broken into four major areas. We'll start with your presentation style. You'll be videotaped a number of times. You'll also gain experience with different training methods. Another segment will address program design and setting objectives. Finally, you'll practice communication skills. You'll have time to practice delivering and receiving feedback."

Expectations (Benefits)

"By the end of the program, you'll have a presentation style that works for you. You'll be more confident and creative as an instructor and you'll communicate ideas and information more consistently and effectively."

Roles

"If you're new to training, you'll learn new concepts and techniques. If you're an experienced instructor, consider this a reinforcement of what you already do well, and an opportunity to fine-tune some skills. The real value is in the sharing of ideas. Please share your experiences with one another. Some of the best ideas come from the group."

Once you've set the stage and delivered your presentation, you're well on your way to a successful outcome.

Checklist for Setting the Stage

DO

- **Consider the type of presentation.** Are you giving a keynote, a seminar, or a one-hour informational session? The type of presentation determines many factors, such as room size, room setup, your presentation style, and whether you'll use visual aids.
- **Determine the audience size.** Size determines the level of intimacy you'll have with your audience, the types of media you'll use, the degree of interaction, and your delivery style.
- **Choose the right room setup.** The room setup is determined by the shape and size of the room, the size of the audience, your purpose, and your style preference. For discussion and interaction, the U-shaped setup is best. Classroom style works for larger groups in which people will be writing. A variation of classroom style is the chevron pattern, in which tables are placed on a diagonal. Team style is perfect for sessions in which the audience will break into frequent subgroups. Theater (auditorium) style is a must for audiences approaching 500 to 1,000. If you're going to be a dinner speaker, banquet style works best, with eight to ten people at a table.

- **Provide food and drinks.** People bond around food. For morning meetings, provide coffee and tea at the very least. It's a good icebreaker, it keeps people awake, and it makes them feel welcome. A few light snacks add to a feeling of hospitality.

- **Start on time.** Don't delay your speech for latecomers. In a large group, ignore latecomers. In a smaller setting, let them know where they can sit. If you don't begin on time, people get restless and you punish the punctual. Also, people will start returning late from breaks if they know you'll wait for them.

- **Take care of housekeeping items early.** Let people know the times for lunch and for taking breaks. Orient them to the rest rooms, the telephones, the support staff, and anything else they need to know.

- **Position your presentation.** Set yourself up for success. Every audience wants to know three things: Who are you? Who are you to tell me? and What's in it for me? Position your presentation by using the BAER formula—**b**ackground, **a**genda, **e**xpectations, **r**oles. This is a very effective approach in training seminars and workshops. Give listeners your background or something personal, tell them your agenda, explain your expectations or the benefits listeners will receive, and tell people what their roles will be—that is, how you'll work together.

- **Arrive early.** Get to the room at least one hour before your presentation. Check the equipment, find the meeting contact, get the feel of the room, and go through a quick rehearsal. Make sure the room is arranged the way you want it. If there are any glitches, you'll have time to correct them.

- **Request a cordless microphone.** For larger audiences, you'll need a microphone. The cordless variety allows you to free your hands. Clip it on to your lapel and turn the battery on when you're ready to speak. Other options: a lavaliere mike goes around your neck and has a long cord. The attached mike keeps you glued to the lectern. Adjust it to the right position and don't lean in to speak. The handheld mike is necessary if you're going to involve the audience and/or you're going to tape them. Practice holding it close enough to pick up your voice but far enough away to avoid sputtering your p's and b's.

- **Mark up your notes.** When you're speaking from a manuscript, triple space the text and use uppercase and lowercase letters. Put a wide border around the text. Use a slash (/) to indicate a pause and a double slash (//) to indicate a long pause. This will help you phrase, pause, and use eye contact. Take a red pencil or yellow highlighter and underline key words. This will create emphasis and vocal variety. Number the pages of your manuscripts or your notecards.

DON'T

- **Hide behind the lectern.** Stand a few inches away from the lectern so that you don't lean on it. Begin your opening remarks in front of the lectern. Stand behind it to use your notes. Build in stories and anecdotes so that you can step out from time to time. The lectern can be a barrier. Be sure to keep your gestures and energy high.

- **Read your notes.** Make eye contact with the audience by keeping your head up and looking at individuals. Reference your notes, pick up a phrase or sentence, and deliver it to the audience.

- **Forget to check the room temperature.** If people are too warm or too cold, they'll fidget and stop listening. Better to make the room a bit on the cool side, since body heat will warm the room. If you see people slumping or clutching their arms, adjust the room temperature.

- **Allow discussions to go on too long.** This is more typical in seminars in which groups discuss the learning objectives. You'll lose the point if you let people ramble on or if the conversation gets off track. Keep discussions focused by bringing people back to your main points.

- **Try to get information from a tired group.** When people are tired, you don't help them by continuing. Give frequent breaks, have people stretch in their seats, and provide some high-energy snacks to revive them. If you're unsure, ask people if they need a break. They'll appreciate your thoughtfulness.
- **Waste time.** Avoid timekillers such as distributing handouts one at a time, starting late, writing every word on a flip chart, and spending too much time on resistant people.

10

Q&A, Difficult People, and Deadly Disasters

Be prepared.
—Boy Scout motto

You're standing behind the podium, grinning like a Cheshire cat, pleased with your performance. The hands go up. The first questioner is rambling and you don't know how to stop him. The next person challenges everything you say. A hostile questioner then lobs a heat-seeking missile: "This stinks." You want to run for cover. If only you could disappear behind the lectern. You wish the stage could just swallow you up.

Ready, aim, fire. No, it's not warfare. It's the question-and-answer period. And if you don't prepare for it, you could feel like a casualty.

What to do? In this chapter, you'll prepare for handling the Q&A period with poise and polish. We'll also discuss how you can recognize and manage a resistant audience, and how you can recover from unexpected disasters you might face.

A Five-Step Process for Handling Questions and Answers

The principles for handling the Q&A period are quite simple. Here's an easy formula to help you remember them—ALRAM:
- **Anticipate and prepare,**
- **Listen,**
- **Repeat or rephrase,**
- **Answer concisely, and**
- **Move on to the next question.**

Anticipate and Prepare

The importance of preparation cannot be overemphasized. Too many speakers spend days and months preparing the speech, only to wing it when it comes to Q&A.

How do you prepare? Simple. Make three lists. The first should contain the questions you know the answers to. Write the questions down and remember your answers. The second list includes the questions whose answers you don't know. Call colleagues or experts to get the answers, or do some additional reading. Finally, the third list contains the questions you dread. These are the controversial questions that you can't avoid. Plan a strategy for handling them.

When Exxon had a large oil spill to contend with, the company couldn't simply deny its involvement. It had to prepare a positive response and demonstrate how it would clean up the spill. By doing a similar type of advance preparation, you'll have the confidence to handle difficult questions and situations. Instead of feeling as if you're in front of a firing range, you'll feel more like you're in a batting cage, able to hit any question that's pitched. You may not always hit a home run, but you'll at least hit the ball. You'll look and feel like a professional.

You also need to consider how you want to handle the Q&A session. Do you want a formal period at the end of your presentation? Or do you want listeners to interject questions at any time? State your preference up front so that your audience will know what to expect. Most formal presentation formats provide time at the end for questions. If you want your session to be interactive, you may choose a different option.

Plan how you'll get the ball rolling for Q&A. What happens if you ask for questions and nobody responds? Most of my students tell me they feel relieved and sit down. But what if you want to encourage questions? Here are some options:

- **Ask the first question yourself.** For example: "A question that is frequently asked is..."
- **Use humor**. "Based on your response, either I did such a good job that there's nothing to ask, or I left you totally confused." Saying this with laughter in your voice and then pausing will sometimes stimulate questions.
- **Plant someone to ask the first question.** Be sure to choose somebody you trust. Otherwise you could get an off-the-wall question that doesn't help your cause. In fact, it's a very good idea to give the person the question you want him or her to ask.

I learned this the hard way. I was giving a ten-minute presentation showcase. I asked a friend if she would ask me a question when I got to the part where I wanted participation. She agreed.

The time arrived and I said, "Would someone like to ask me a question?" I waited but no response was forthcoming. I kept looking at my friend. Still no response. Someone finally felt sorry for me and asked a question. After the presentation, I approached my friend and said, "What happened? I thought you were going to ask a question. Did you forget?" She replied, "No, I just couldn't think of a good one." Don't let this happen to you. If you plant a person in the audience, write down the question for him or her.

- **Distribute index cards.** Tell people to write their questions down. Take a short break to collect the cards or have people pass the cards forward. This method guarantees that you get questions. A side benefit: if you have a hostile audience, you get to choose the questions to answer.

Listen

This book devotes an entire chapter (Chapter 4) to listening because it's so important. Listening is especially critical during Q&A. You need to listen both physically and mentally during Q&A. You listen physically by focusing your energy and planting your feet. Don't lapse into sloppy habits, like pacing or fidgeting. This sends a negative message. If someone asks you a tough question, you don't want to start backing up defensively. Hold your ground.

You also need to listen mentally. Listen to the person's entire message before you answer. Even if you can anticipate the question, hold your tongue until the person finishes. You had your turn to speak. Now it's someone else's turn. If you cut people off to answer their questions, you'll be perceived as rude and uncaring. And if someone changes direction in the middle of his or her question, you could find yourself answering the wrong question.

Repeat or Rephrase

This takes some practice to remember. Most beginning speakers forget to repeat the question and begin answering as if they were in a private conversation. A mental shift has to take place. The question isn't yours—it belongs to the group. If you don't repeat the question, others may not hear it, and you risk losing people. They many even begin side-talking as they try to figure out what was said.

You can repeat basic questions verbatim. Suppose someone asks, "How long does this process take?"

You can say, "The question is, 'How long does this process take?'" It's that simple.

But what if someone makes a statement instead of asking a question?

You have two options. Either you can ask the person to rephrase the statement as a question, or you can turn the statement into a question yourself.

For example, if someone says, "It's not practical. It will take too long and we don't have a track record for this kind of project." You say, "What is your question?" or "The question is, 'Is it practical?'" (Note: it isn't necessary to always use the carrier phrase, "The question is..." It can begin to sound monotonous after a while. If the question is about cost, you can vary it by saying, "The gentleman asked about cost" or "What is the cost?" or "The question concerns the cost...")

When do you repeat the question? Always if you're speaking to a large group. For crowds of 50 to 100, it's still a good idea to repeat questions. You don't need to repeat the questions if:
- You're in a one-to-one meeting,
- You're in a small group,
- You're in a training seminar (unless it's a very large group), or
- The questions are hostile.

When you get a hostile question, don't repeat it. Doing so will only give power to negative language. Don't reinforce the negativity. Neutralize the acid by rephrasing the question.

For example, suppose someone jeers, "I heard your company really screwed up. How do we know you won't screw us too?" Don't repeat the question, but don't ignore it either or people will think your company really isn't reputable. Instead, rephrase the question more positively: "The question is, 'How have we learned from our mistakes and how will that benefit you in the future?'"

Don't get defensive, and do not go head-to-head with the heckler. If you do either, you'll be playing the heckler's game—and you will lose. You may also risk alienating the rest of the group. It's easier to handle one hothead than to stir up a nest of vipers. A better option is to stay calm, cool, and collected.

Frequently, others in the group will help you out. It's an interesting law of group dynamics. If you remain non-defensive, the group will come to your aid. When a heckler becomes relentless, the group will often turn to the troublemaker and say, "Sit down. Give someone else a chance to ask a question." Or people may raise their hands to agree with you instead of the heckler. Never underestimate the power of peer pressure.

Case Study

In one of my public speaking seminars, the students were practicing how to handle questions and answers. One woman from the Florida hospitality industry was trying to persuade a group of tourists to visit the Miami area. She painted an enticing scene and built a convincing case for choosing Miami as a vacation spot.

During the Q&A segment, she was confronted about an incident. The news media had reported that a child had been killed by an alligator. In an attempt to use rephrasing, she replied, "The question concerns an incident where an alligator had a problem with a child...." The entire class burst into side-splitting laughter. She realized too late how silly that sounded. Fortunately, it was a only training session. Use rephrasing when appropriate, but acknowledge reality.

One cautionary note about this process: be realistic. If a tragedy or disaster has occurred and people confront you about it, acknowledge it.

Answer Concisely

The Q&A session is not the time to give a doctoral dissertation. Keep your answers short and to the point. And answer to the

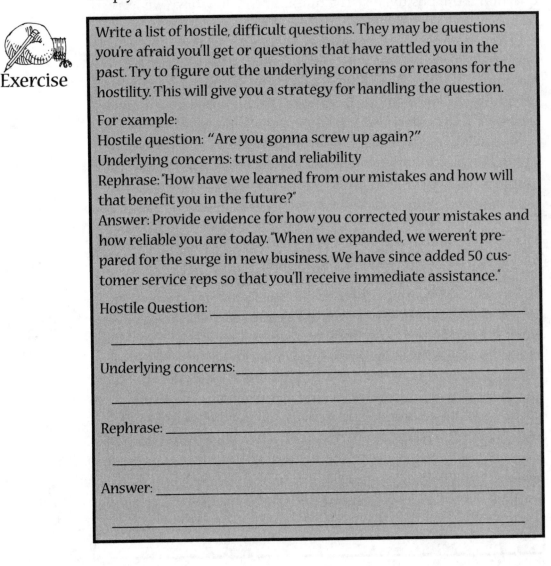

Exercise

Write a list of hostile, difficult questions. They may be questions you're afraid you'll get or questions that have rattled you in the past. Try to figure out the underlying concerns or reasons for the hostility. This will give you a strategy for handling the question.

For example:
Hostile question: "Are you gonna screw up again?"
Underlying concerns: trust and reliability
Rephrase: "How have we learned from our mistakes and how will that benefit you in the future?"
Answer: Provide evidence for how you corrected your mistakes and how reliable you are today. "When we expanded, we weren't prepared for the surge in new business. We have since added 50 customer service reps so that you'll receive immediate assistance."

Hostile Question: _____

_____

Underlying concerns: _____

_____

Rephrase: _____

_____

Answer: _____

_____

group. This requires a mental shift on your part. Most of us answer directly to the person who asked the question. But in large groups, you must answer to the group. Make eye contact with the person who posed the question, then look at other individuals in the room. If you only answer to one person, the rest of the audience may tune out. Remember: it's the group's question.

What if you don't know the answer? For starters, don't fake it! If someone does know the answer and challenges you, then what? You instantly lose credibility. A better option is to admit you don't know and offer to get back to the group: "I'm not sure about that. Let me check it and get back to you." People don't expect you to have every answer.

Another option is to defer to an expert in the room. If your manager or co-worker can answer the question, you can say, "Jane is the expert in that area" or "Bill, do you want to answer that?" The disadvantage of this technique is that you can lose control. So be sure you can trust that expert, and know when to cut back in.

If the answer to the question is confidential, don't give it to the audience. Stand your ground. "That's confidential, and I'm not at liberty to discuss it." As long as you're consistent in your response, the audience will respect you.

Move on to the Next Question

The last step in handling the Q&A session is important in helping you maintain control. Answer to the entire group, but end your answer by speaking to someone other than the original questioner.

How do you do this? As you're answering to the group, you'll see other hands raised. Or you might pick up body language cues that someone else has a question. When you finish your answer, finish by focusing on someone other than the questioner.

Why? Because if you go back to that person, he or she will ask another question.

What's wrong with that? Nothing, really. But you don't want to get into an ongoing dialogue. You'll lose time, you'll lose the interest of the group, and you may lose control. By ending on a different person, you keep the process going. You send a message that everyone has an opportunity to be heard.

This is especially important with difficult people. If you end your eye contact with a new person, the difficult questioner has less of an opportunity to break in or dominate. You've already engaged a new questioner. The hostile person who wants to zing it to you will have a harder time because now he's interfering with someone else. That other person is going to tell the hostile person to back down and give someone else a chance.

Another technique is to use physical movement. Start walking in the opposite direction of the hostile questioner, finish your answer by speaking to someone new, and say, "Next question?" Once you look back, the hostile person will try to unnerve you again. But shouldn't you check back for understanding? No. That's a good communication technique, but it's not always effective in Q&A sessions. If you didn't answer the question, the audience will let you know.

Finally, the end is drawing near. Don't end abruptly. Let the audience know you're wrapping up. Tell the audience you have time for a few more questions and then bring the session to an end. The best way to end is to reinforce your message. People will remember the last thing they hear. So summarize your message. You have a selling opportunity. Even if you're giving a monthly update, here's one more instance to drive home the information. So take advantage.

Recap your main points and leave listeners with an action to take or some food for thought. For example: "In summary, we've discussed the importance of completing the claims correctly. We've reviewed the process for receiving the information, printing legibly in black ink, and proofing the claim before submitting it to the next level. I'd like to leave you with this thought: We can save time and expense by doing it right the first time every time. The goal is to see that every team earns a quality award. You've got the tools. See you at the top!"

Signs of Resistance

What if you're going to spend some significant time with your audience? If you're going to be giving a seminar or a training class, you need to be prepared on a different level. You'll have much more interaction with the group. There will be a constant exchange of ideas, an ongoing give-and-take. And that can spell trouble if you don't know how to handle group dynamics.

The first question you need to ask is, "Why are the audience members here?" If you're conducting an in-house corporate seminar, the answer is usually "Because attendance is required." Uh-oh. You have your work cut out for you. You've just entered the resistance zone.

How do you know when your audience is resistant? Here are a few signs:

- Excessive questioning,
- Questions set up to trap you,
- Closed body language (arms folded across chest),
- Side conversations,
- Silence,
- Listeners looking at their watches,
- Listeners reading the paper,
- Listeners changing the subject,
- Fidgeting, and
- Difficulty understanding your instructions.

It's one thing to recognize resistance. It's quite another to figure out why it's there and how to deal with it.

Here's a simple formula to help you understand why your audience members are resistant. It's called How to/Chance to/ Want to:

- Is the reason for the resistance a lack of *know-how*? If an individual is avoiding your instructions, it may be due to fear or inexperience. Maybe the person is afraid of looking foolish. Perhaps there's a literacy problem or a language barrier. The solution is to show the person *how*. Give the listener the support and tools to go to the next step.
- Is the reason for the resistance a lack of *opportunity*? If a person isn't participating and there are many verbal people in the group, he or she may not have a chance to respond to all those extroverts. The solution is to provide a *chance*. Change the group. Ask people to write down their responses. Call on quiet people.
- Is the reason for the resistance a lack of motivation? If the person is saying, "I don't have time" or "I already know that," he or she may not want to do what you're asking. The solution is to provide value to make the person *want* what you're providing. Explain the benefits.

Managing Difficult People

Your work isn't over once you've managed resistance in the audience. Audiences come to you with their own emotional baggage, most of which has nothing to do with you. But somehow their needs aren't being met.

So who is this cast of characters, and how do you handle them?

Eager Beaver. This person is always the first to raise his or her hand. The Eager Beaver is very interested and eager to participate. He or she makes you feel good. But nobody else is responding while the Eager Beaver is furiously waving at you for attention. Handle the Eager Beaver by acknowledging his or her responses. You don't want to dampen enthusiasm. Then suggest that others participate. For example: "That's a good point, Joe.

What does everyone else think? Let's get some other opinions."

Negative Nellie. This person is very resistant and will challenge everything. If everyone else sees the silver lining, Negative Nellie will find the cloud. Ignoring this person usually doesn't work. Take a more direct approach. Confront Negative Nellie head on. Grab a flip chart and start charting the person's concerns. When you have all of the issues, offer a couple of options. Deal with them immediately or later. You can take one issue at a time, address it, and cross it off the list. Or you can say you'll take the issues back to the powers that be to discuss changes. Either way, you're dealing with the issues and getting people focused on solutions.

Whiner. This person loves to complain, but he or she is different from Negative Nellie. Whiners aren't necessarily resistant to learning, but they complain about everything: the room is too hot, there's not enough light, there aren't enough breaks, etc. Whiners are formidable fault finders but will offer no solutions. This is a no-win situation. Acknowledge their comments and ask the group for solutions. Don't try to win them over. If they complain that it's too cold, ask the group if they agree and offer to check it out on the next break. Don't get into a debate with them.

Expert. There are two kinds of experts: the real thing and the know-it-all. What the expert really needs is recognition for his or her achievements and knowledge. So do that! Call on experts early and ask for their opinions. Play to their experience: "Sue, you've been doing this a long time. What's your view?" Don't let their expertise intimidate you. Encourage them and they will become your greatest allies. For know-it-alls (people who think they're experts), acknowledge their opinions and ask the group for alternatives. Don't get into a debate.

Dominator. This person wants control. He or she can intimidate you and the group. Handle dominators by summarizing their viewpoints and asking the group for their opinions. Humor can work: "Let's hear from someone other than Bill." If nothing is working, call a break and speak to the dominator privately. Ask for his or her help: "I'm concerned that the group isn't participating. Will you help me out? Don't answer any questions and let's see if that gets them talking."

Clown. The clown is constantly joking. This can be disruptive and inappropriate. Speak to clowns privately and ask them to hold the jokes. During the session, be very serious in the face of their joking.

Inarticulate. People who are shy or who have difficulty expressing themselves need some extra handholding. Paraphrase your understanding of what they say and give them extra time to formulate a thought. When they know the topic, call on them to build their confidence.

Dependent. This person may not seem to be a problem because he or she is always agreeable. In reality, however, this person lacks confidence. Help dependents by asking them easy questions. Praise their contributions and be available to assist them when necessary.

Rambler. Here's the quintessential storyteller. You ask ramblers the time and they tell you the history of watchmaking. Ramblers go off on tangents. So help them out. Cut in and repeat what you think the question is. Then begin to answer it: "As I understand you, Judy, you're asking about the philosophy of time management." Don't let ramblers go on and on and on.

Withdrawn. These people don't participate. Their bodies are there but you don't know if their minds are. Withdrawn people may feel intimidated or bored. So begin by determining the reason for their silence. If you sense that withdrawn types are timid, build their confidence and call on them for easy topics. If they're bored, involve them by asking for their opinions.

Poor Loser. The poor loser can't admit a mistake. So don't push. Let poor losers save face. Acknowledge a difference of opinion. Agree to disagree. You can also ask questions—for example: "How did you arrive at that?" or "Help me understand your thinking." You can then find some area you both can agree upon: "I can see how you would arrive at that conclusion." This technique is especially helpful when dealing with multicultural audiences who value saving face.

Off Tracker. When someone in the group digresses from the main objectives and begins chatting socially, bring the person back to focus. Acknowledge what he or she said and direct it back to the learning objectives.

Side Talkers. In a large auditorium you can ignore side conversations. But in a smaller group, side conversations can be disruptive. There are three techniques you can use to regain control:

1. Be silent. Stop talking and look in the side talkers' direction. Once it gets quiet they will look up and stop talking.
2. Confront side talkers directly: "Was there a question?"
3. Use the walk technique. Keep talking, walk toward the side talkers, and continue speaking while standing in front of them. They'll get the message.

Physical Distractors. People who tap pencils, kick chairs, or talk on a cellular phone can distract the group. Use body language and eye contact to call attention to their behavior. Ignore it if it doesn't bother anyone.

More Tips for Managing Difficult People

Use humor. Humor is the best deflector of hostility and negativity. You can't be angry when you're laughing. Humor can also help people save face. Humor is not joke-telling. Don't put down participants. Self-deprecating humor works well. Use the humor of the group if you're not naturally funny. Study other trainers and

Exercise

Which difficult personality most irritates you? _____
_____
Why? _____
_____
Who does this person remind you of? _____
What response does it trigger in you? _____
_____
What will you do to minimize your reaction next time you
encounter this personality? _____
_____

borrow a few of their lines. If someone walks out in the middle of your lecture, you can say, "Oh, look, my first walking ovation."

Avoid power struggles. This is a win-lose proposition. You can win. They can lose. But even if you win, you lose because you can create enemies. Acknowledge people's feelings: "I hear what you're saying." Ask for more information. Paraphrase your understanding. Offer to discuss the conflict later.

Show that you care. Get to know people before, during, and after the breaks. Ask how they're doing. Offer your help. Find common ground. It's difficult to be hostile to someone who sincerely cares about you.

Let the group help you. It's a law of group dynamics that if you stay non-defensive, the group will come to your rescue. If an individual is complaining and resisting, ask the group for input: "Is everyone too warm?" "Should we eliminate this activity?" "Do you agree that this method can't work here?" The resisting or complaining person will back down under peer pressure.

Involve everyone. Break participants into small groups to minimize complaining and dominating. Keep changing the groups to change the dynamics.

Don't take resistance personally. Resistance usually has little to do with you. People come with their own agendas, fears, and emotional needs. The best strategy is to remove your ego from the relationship. Figure out what the resistant person needs and then provide it.

Disaster Recovery

Every so often, Murphy's Law will take full effect. You must be prepared for these situations. Identify what could happen and then plan what to do about it.

Most situations are minor mishaps you can manage—unlike the speaker whose half slip fell down in the middle of her speech. She couldn't pull it up because she would have to lift her dress. So she simply stepped out of it. An embarrassing event indeed. This kind of thing isn't likely to happen to you. But it's still good to be prepared.

Here are some potentially embarrassing moments you should be aware of and some ways for dealing with them should they occur:

You lose your train of thought and freeze up. This usually happens when you're not prepared. To prevent it:
- Be sure to practice out loud and time yourself.
- Don't write a word-for-word script. Memorize concepts, not words.
- Use handouts and talk from the same handout the audience has. This keeps you on track and allows you to write additional prompts for yourself.
- Create overheads or slides. Bullet points become your notes so that you always know where you are.

- Stay calm and don't panic. If you forget a point, the audience won't know. Carry on.
- If you're totally lost, do an interactive exercise. Ask the audience members to pair up and discuss a point you just made. This will give you three to five minutes to find your place and collect your thoughts.
- Ask the audience to help you out. Say, "This is a test. Who remembers the last point I made?" Or, "All together now. What are the five steps to good customer service?" As people are reciting, you'll gain thinking time.

You lose your material or forget to bring it. You find that you've left your notes or an important part of your presentation at home or at the office. To prevent this from happening and being stuck with nothing:

- Send an extra copy of your presentation to the meeting planner or a contact at the site.
- Always check your materials the night before and once again before you leave.
- Never check your presentation material with your baggage. It should be part of your carry-on luggage.
- Stay in touch with your office. People there may be able to e-mail or fax you a copy of your talk.
- Improvise. If you can't get to your notes, talk from experience. Jot down some notes and outline your most memorable lessons.
- Start a dialogue. Change the nature of your presentation. Open with an objective and a few points and then have an open dialogue with the audience. They'll appreciate having their questions answered. For example: "Instead of me lecturing, I thought we would make this session interactive. I know you have a lot of questions and experiences to share and we want to hear from you today." Then break listeners into rows or subgroups and have them discuss a point.

- Be creative. I was once going to coach a senior executive. I left my house in my running shoes only to discover that I had put in my briefcase only one shoe from the pair of leather pumps I was going to wear for the coaching session. When I got to the office, I realized I couldn't meet the executive in my running shoes. I remembered that one of the sales reps kept extra shoes in her file drawer. I took a pair of shoes from the drawer and stuffed the toes with paper. (Her foot was much bigger than mine.) If there hadn't been any shoes available, I would have used humor.

You tell a joke and nobody laughs. To prevent this from happening:
- Prepare and practice out loud. Try the joke or humor on others. Make sure it plays well and doesn't offend anyone.
- Give people time to laugh. Pause and expect a response.
- Make sure the joke is relevant to the topic. Set it up properly.
- If the joke bombs, have a comeback line: "You had to be there." "Let's have a moment of silence for the joke that just died."

The audience is silent. A lack of response from audience members could mean that they're not comfortable with themselves. If so:
- Try an interactive activity early on to break the ice. Get people to talk to a partner about a point you just made. For example: "You'll have two minutes to tell your partner about your best sale and your worst sale." Or, "In two minutes, tell the person next to you your most difficult job or challenge." Once they're finished talking to each other, ask them to report back to you and the others.
- When you ask a question and get no response, try humor. Nod and shake your head and say, "This means yes and this means no." Or, "Have I totally confused you?"
- Try rephrasing the question more simply. The audience may not have understood.
- Be silent and wait for five seconds. If you continually answer

your own questions, your audience will sit back and let you do the work. Silence is uncomfortable and will often compel someone to respond.

- Call on someone, but let the audience know you're going to do this. Choose someone who looks outgoing and don't embarrass anyone.

Your microphone doesn't work. To prevent this from happening or deal with it when it does happen:

- Arrive early and check the microphone. Practice speaking into it to avoid feedback. Find the on/off switch. Ask for an additional microphone as a backup.
- Don't begin until the sound system is working. Let the meeting planner handle it.
- Call a break if the system cuts out during your speech.
- Use humor if you get feedback noise. Memorize one-liners that get a laugh.

Your presentation is cut short. To be sure you can deal with this effectively:

- Always have a short and long version of your speech. You'll be prepared if you're told you have less time. I can give the same presentation in a half day, one hour, thirty minutes, and ten minutes.
- Memorize your main points. Give the audience your points but offer fewer examples, stories, and embellishments. This will cut down on your time significantly.
- If you have a one-hour talk that has been cut to 15 minutes, use humor and offer to give people the highlights. Tell them that they can find additional information in their handouts. Offer your phone number and agree to answer questions by telephone. Don't let people know that you're upset. Be poised and professional.
- Stage a Q&A session: "Since we don't have much time, I'd like to review what's happening in technology and then open it up

for questions. In a nutshell.....” People will at least feel they had an opportunity to ask for specific information.

You trip over a wire or while walking to the platform. To deal with this:

- Change your thinking. Don't panic. Everyone stumbles once in a while.
- Make light of the mishap: “I want you to know I've been practicing that entrance for weeks.” Or, “Never let it be said that I don't know how to make an entrance.” You'll probably get a laugh and relax both yourself and the audience.

The first speaker told your story or exercise or example. To prevent this or deal with it when it happens:

- Contact other speakers on the program and discuss your content. Preparation is the best defense.
- Find out how many people heard the first speaker. Ask those people to stand and try the exercise on them.
- Use the story or example as a learning tool. Review in your own words what the previous speaker said: “How many of you remember Maureen's story about leadership? What happened at the end?” This technique will give you audience participation. It will also serve as a review and endear you to the other speaker. You'll sound smooth and professional in your ability to integrate another speaker's content into yours.
- Plan more than one story or exercise. If someone tells story A, you tell story B. This happened to me one time. The lunchtime keynote speaker used the exact opening exercise that I had planned to use in my breakout session. So I switched to another exercise. I was really glad I'd heard his speech.
- If you give the same example without knowing it was just used, make a joke about the “brilliance of like minds.” Or, joke about being from the same “speakers school.” Stay poised and laugh at yourself.

People arrive or return late. To deal with this or prevent it from happening:

- Don't embarrass the people. Point out any empty seats and continue your presentation.
- In a large auditorium, ignore latecomers.
- If someone is an hour late, ask him or her to pair up with someone else to catch up.
- Ask people to return promptly from breaks. Do this during the opening of your seminar or presentation. Explain why it's important: "We have a tight program today. Please get back on time so that we can cover all the material. I'm committed to getting you out on time." That last line usually works. Nobody wants the program to run late.
- Ask yourself if you're really adding value. If people don't see the relevance of your presentation, they won't want to return for more.
- If a large portion of your audience is returning late, you have a problem. Deal with it directly by asking for feedback. Perhaps there was a company announcement that's upsetting people. Maybe they have to make their quota this week and don't want to be at your presentation. Negotiate with your listeners. Maybe they need a longer break or lunch hour in order to get their work done.
- If you're presenting to a sales group, understand that those people may have important calls to make. Be sure management supports the seminar and insist on having your program off-site. If people can return to their desks, you may never get them back.
- Appoint a monitor. Ask if someone will round up people at the given time.
- Go outside and let people know you're ready to get started. It's easy for listeners to lose track of the time.
- Be specific and synchronize your watches: "Let's break for ten minutes and get back at 10:45."

The audience doesn't want to be there. This can be one of the worst nightmares for a speaker. To deal with it:

- Find out why people don't want to be present. Do your homework first. Ask the manager or host why people are coming to your presentation. Learn about your listeners' attitudes. Forewarned is forearmed.
- Be sure to sell the audience on the benefits your presentation will bring to them and their job. Do this right up front before you begin speaking.
- If you expect resistance, address it at the beginning. Your listeners may need a few minutes to vent. Go around the room and ask volunteers to tell you how they're feeling and what they would like to get out of your program. Let them express their feelings but keep them focused on the positive.
- Use humor. Ask people, "Why are you here, other than 'my boss sent me'?"

Checklist for Handling Q and A, Difficult People, and Disasters

DO

- **Prepare recovery strategies.** Anticipate what could go wrong. What if you trip over a cord, people arrive late, the equipment malfunctions, or you tell a joke and nobody laughs? When Murphy's Law is in operation, levity is in order. Laugh at yourself. If the machine isn't working, call a short break. If you're not upset, the audience won't be either.
- **Stimulate questions.** Open the Q&A session with "What questions do you have?" If nobody responds, ask the first question yourself or plant someone in the audience. You can also ask people to write questions on index cards and hand them in after the formal presentation.
- **Listen to the entire question.** Let the person finish his or her

question before you start answering it. Listening is a form of respect. The exception to this rule is when someone is rambling. Help the person by cutting in and paraphrasing.

- **Repeat the question.** Every question is the group's question. In a large audience, you must repeat the question or you risk losing the group. This is especially important when you're being taped. The tape will not pick up the question if the person asking it isn't talking into a microphone.
- **Turn statements into questions.** If someone says, "We can't afford it," say, "The question is, 'Can we afford it?'"
- **Rephrase the question.** When the question is unclear or hostile, take the sting out of it by paraphrasing it in positive language. "What the blank could you tell us about managing?" is rephrased as, "The question is, 'What is my experience?'"
- **Answer to the entire group.** If you answer only to the person who asked the question, you will create a dialogue and lose the group's attention. Make eye contact with the entire group.
- **Answer concisely.** Be direct, simple, and concise. Don't pontificate. People have already heard your presentation. Get to the point.
- **End your answer by speaking to the next questioner.** Use eye contact to find the next questioner. This technique will help you avoid being entrapped by a hostile questioner. If you finish the answer on the questioner, he or she will simply ask you another question.
- **Physically get away from a hostile questioner.** Shift your eye contact to someone else and move to another part of the room. This method will let you disengage yourself from the hostile questioner.
- **Manage difficult personalities.** Determine the type of personality of the person causing the problem and address the underlying need. For experts or know-it-alls, the underlying need is recognition. So give it to them. Call on them early or ask for their opinions. Satisfy the underlying need and you'll

be able to manage the behavior.
- **End Q&A with a summary.** People remember the last thing they hear, so bring back your summary and action step. Remind them of why they were there. A summary will reinforce your message.

DON'T
- **Wing it.** Anticipate the questions and prepare three lists:
    1. Questions whose answers you know, then rehearse.
    2. Questions whose answers you don't know, then research.
    3. Questions that are sensitive or controversial or ones that you dread, then plan a strategy.
- **Get defensive.** No matter what a hostile questioner does, stay in control. Generally the group will come to your defense.
- **Evaluate the question.** Once you say, "Good question," you risk offending people who didn't ask a good question. Stay neutral and repeat questions without evaluating them.
- **Use sarcasm or belittling comments.** "As I said before…," "There's a real brain teaser," "That's an obvious question," and similar remarks put down the questioner.
- **Fake it.** If you don't know the answer, admit it. Offer to get back to the questioner. You will lose credibility if you're wrong and someone exposes you.
- **Go over the time limit.** Respect people's schedules and make yourself available to talk to individuals after your presentation is over.

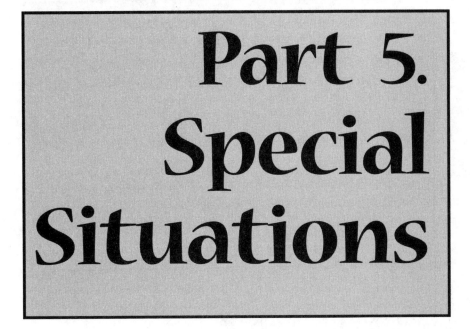

Part 5.
Special
Situations

Special Speaking
Situations

Life is a presentation.
–Diane DiResta

I keep saying that everyone is a public speaker. Even if you've never made a formal presentation and you never will, you may still find yourself in a special situation in which you have to speak before an audience. You may have to introduce a speaker, manage a trade show booth, or chair a meeting. You can prepare for these situations and others by learning a few simple principles. In this chapter we will address:

- Making an introduction,
- Leaving a voice mail message,
- Presenting at a trade show,
- Doing team presentations,
- Chairing a meeting,
- Giving a motivational keynote,
- Conducting seminars and workshops,
- Doing one-to-one presentations,
- Delivering sales presentations,
- Making impromptu presentations,
- Participating in media interviews, and
- Videoconferencing.

Special situations call for special measures. These quick tips will ensure that you know what to do.

Making an Introduction

When you're introducing a speaker, here are some simple strategies to consider:

- Be prepared. How you introduce a speaker sets the tone. Don't wing it.
- Ask the speaker for a short, written introduction. (An introduction is different from a biography.) Read the introduction the way the speaker requests.
- If there is no introduction, request a bio and ask the speaker what he or she wants said.
- KISS—Keep it short and simple. Your introduction should take one minute or less.
- Structure the introduction like any other presentation.
- A good introduction has a beginning, a middle, and an end. Use the TEPS formula: topic, experience, personalize, speaker's name. Present the title or topic, cite the experience or credentials of the presenter, tell the audience something to humanize the speaker, and end with the speaker's name.

Personalize your introduction by mentioning how you know the speaker. The audience wants to know the person as well as the topic: "We met at the last conference. She was so dynamic that I just had to ask her to give the keynote this year."

- Don't tell personal stories about the speaker that could cause embarrassment. No surprises.
- Don't tell jokes unless you first check with the speaker.
- Practice pronouncing the speaker's name. If it's a difficult name, write it out phonetically so that you can say it correctly.
- End with the speaker's name: "Please help me welcome Steven Speaker...." People will remember the last thing they hear. They may forget the presenter's name if you don't mention it at the end of your introduction.

Leaving a Voice Mail Message

Why is voice mail included in our discussion? Because voice mail is a presentation. If you make a negative first impression by telephone, you may cause a potential customer, vendor, employer, or date to hang up. One young manager left such long, unfocused voice mails that her boss told her to call and redo them. She then sent the manager to a presentation skills class.

Do you want people to return your calls? Then let your voice message leave a positive imprint by following these guidelines:

- Prepare your message. Think it through and jot down a few bullet points. It's irritating to listen to someone collect his or her thoughts out loud.
- Get to the point. Focus your message. What is it that you want and by when? Boil it down to the facts. A stream of consciousness approach is not effective.
- KISS—Keep it short and simple. Remember: people are busy. They don't want to sift through a lot of information to get your point.
- Don't have a conversation with the machine. (I had a friend

who called three times in order to finish her message.) The purpose of voice mail is to get the person to call you back or to leave information that the person requested.

- Monitor your tone. The listener can't respond to body language, so your tone of voice and words play a more important role. Don't leave a message when you're upset. The listener will hear the edge in your tone. Pause and calm yourself.
- Speak slowly and pause. Voice mail is not a race. There have been so many times when I could not understand the person's name. Other times, the speaker gave the phone number so quickly that I had to play the message twice in order to write it down. Pause to separate number groups: "My number is 800 (pause) 123 (pause) 4567."
- Enunciate clearly. Sloppy speech leaves a lasting impression. When recruiting job candidates, employers often eliminate people over the phone. Why lose out on a job, a sale, or an opportunity because of a negative impression? Many telephones are imperfect filters that distort sounds. Talk into the receiver, sit up straight, and project your voice.
- Tell the person how to reach you. This will prevent telephone tag: "I'm out of the office but will be returning by 3:00. The best time to reach me is between 3:30 and 5:00. If we don't connect, you can reach me by e-mail."
- Always leave your telephone number. The person you called may be out of the office when retrieving messages and may not have your phone number handy.

Presenting at a Trade Show

The most common mistake presenters make at trade shows is not realizing that they're actually making a presentation. They treat the time behind the booth as an opportunity to "schmooze" and "booze." While there can be some fun networking parties, this is a serious selling situation. Trade show selling is rated as second to advertising in effectiveness. So make the most of this gold mine:

- Define your purpose. Why are you there? To conduct market research? To size up the competition? To introduce new products? To generate leads? You're all at the same show, but you may have different reasons for exhibiting. Defining your purpose will give you a clear focus for the day.

- Project the right image. Are you upscale? Small but friendly? Specially priced? Cutting-edge? Once you all agree on the organization's image, define your behaviors and act accordingly. For example, Mercedes dealers wear pinstripe suits. That wouldn't fit if you were selling Hyundais.

- Set goals. Be specific. "To generate 25 new leads for hotel rooms by December 2" is measurable and specific. By having a purpose and a goal, you'll be able to measure and modify your results.

- Organize the booth. Rid the booth of clutter. If you have several handouts, place them out of view, away from key brochures. You can pull them out if needed. Leave space on the table. Don't drink coffee or eat snacks while you're in the booth; it creates an unprofessional look. Take a break if you need to. Also, don't read the newspaper during down time. All eyes are on you.

- Polish your presentation. Greet each person with a smile, a firm handshake, and direct eye contact. Nobody wants to buy from someone with a weak handshake whose darting eyes are looking for the next lead. Project warmth and enthusiasm. Take short notes when talking to a prospect. Don't chew gum, smoke, or chat with co-workers while you're in the booth. And never leave the booth unattended.

- Put your best foot forward. It's best to stand in front of the booth. That makes it easier to greet customers. Sitting will make you look too casual and not ready to do business.

- Promote the booth. To increase traffic at your booth, don't leave things to chance. Send qualified prospects a special invitation to receive promotional material. You can also advertise, send direct mail, or do public relations and telemarketing. Schedule appointments to meet with existing customers. (You can often purchase member mailing lists.) Sponsor a fun event at your booth, such as roulette or golf, and watch the crowds gather.

- Don't give away the store. Instead of handing bagsful of premiums to everyone who walks buy, ask for business cards. Keep premiums on the back table behind the booth. When someone comes by, ask if he or she would like a free gift in exchange for a business card. Your goal is to obtain leads.

- Proactively prospect. Capitalize on every chance to make contacts. That means getting out from the booth and going to where the customers are. Network at every opportunity. Set up breakfast or lunch meetings. Attend evening networking events. Walk around the floor. Talk to people during coffee breaks. Attend educational seminars. It's easier to make a sale when people are relaxed.

- Prepare an opening line. There is no greater waste of time than talking to a non-buyer. But trade show presenters continually fall into this trap. Cut to the chase with an opening line: "Are you a meeting planner?" "Do you purchase computers?" "Are you a purchasing agent?" "Do you book hotels?" If the answer is yes, you can continue to chat. Otherwise, thank the person and politely send him or her on. Your goal is to gain qualified leads and convert them into sales.

- Listen, listen, listen. According to Allen Konopacki of Incomm Research, the No. 1 reason customers don't buy is because the salesperson didn't listen. If you listen actively and with all of your senses, you'll gain a major advantage over your competition. Most of your competitors will be too busy talking. But people don't want to hear a sales pitch. They want their needs met. Listening and questioning skills close sales.

Doing Team Presentations

Team selling is becoming more popular. As technology and new products are rapidly developed, one person can no longer be the expert. That means technical specialists or subject matter experts must be part of the presentation.

Another form of team presenting is the panel discussion. At industry conferences, you may be asked to be part of a panel to discuss a particular issue. Or you may be asked to discuss your job at an employee orientation program.

Here are some guidelines to keep in mind when you're presenting as a team:

- Act like a team. Your presentation should flow smoothly, with everyone working together. This isn't the time to upstage others and compete for the spotlight.
- Prepare. Meet beforehand to discuss roles, timing, and the general process. Agree on how you'll handle difficult questions or situations that might arise.
- Appoint a leader or moderator. In the case of a sales presentation, the leader is generally the account representative. In a panel discussion, the moderator acts as a facilitator and does not present. The objective is to keep things moving.
- Decide on each person's role. Who will speak on which topic, and for how long?
- Plan your agenda. The leader generally opens the presentation by introducing the team members and their topics. He or she then explains how the presentation will proceed: "First we will discuss the background history, then the current state of affairs, and finally we will make some future projections." The audience needs an agenda to understand what you'll be presenting. The agenda serves as a road map.
- Plan the transitions. To create a smooth flow, team members must segue from their material and turn the floor over to the next presenter: "That covers taxes. Now Ray will talk to you

about estate planning."

- Time each segment and rehearse out loud. Good presenters finish on time. If you're given ten minutes, stick to the agreement. The only way to stay on time is to practice out loud and time yourself.
- Look at the audience, not your teammates. You need to watch the nonverbals of your audience. You can't do that if you're watching the speaker or your teammates. It also looks more professional for the team to be looking in the same direction: toward the audience. Remember: all eyes are on you, and not just when it's your turn to speak. If you look bored, chew gum, or tap your pencil, you will create a negative impression.
- Don't debate or interrupt when someone is speaking. If a speaker omits vital information, wait until he or she is finished and then say, "If I may add to what John just said..." or "To piggyback on what Carol said earlier..."
- Plan the closing. At the end, the leader announces the question-and-answer session and keeps things on track. Summarize and end with a positive message: "That concludes our presentation. We've discussed investments, taxes, and estate planning. We leave you with this thought: it's never too early to start planning for retirement."

Chairing a Meeting

Chairing a meeting is somewhat different from a team presentation. In a meeting, every team member may participate equally, and the goals of meetings and team presentations differ.

Your role as meeting chair is to facilitate. You must be a catalyst and get others to offer information and share ideas. Keep these points in mind when you're chairing a meeting:

- Know why you're holding the meeting. What outcome are you

trying to achieve? This will keep you focused and purposeful.
- Clarify your role as chair. How do the participants perceive you? Did you call the meeting? Do participants report to you? If you're the boss, people may be scared to speak their minds. If you're not the boss, what do people expect from you as the chair?
- Set a positive tone early in the meeting. Greet people before you sit down. Break the ice with some light humor to relax the group. People are often tentative and guarded during the first few minutes. Provide coffee if appropriate. People bond around food and drink.
- Provide a written agenda on a handout or flip chart. The agenda keeps the meeting on track. Let the group know the time frame and guidelines for working together: "We have only forty minutes today. I will update you on the customer service situation, and then I'd like us to brainstorm some solutions to the challenges we face."
- Start on time. Don't wait for stragglers. If you begin and end on time, you'll condition people to be prompt.
- Create interest with an enticing title. Instead of a management topic about "Business Etiquette," title it "What's Rudeness Costing You?"
- Appoint a person to take minutes so that you can later review discussions that took place and the decisions that were made.
- Manage the group dynamics. Don't let one person dominate. Ask for other opinions. If some people are silent, draw them out by asking for their thoughts.
- Handle conflicts impartially. Encourage cooperation by clarifying what people have said and then asking the participants to propose solutions. Heated arguments may require a timeout in which group members take a short break and return when they've cooled off.
- Assign a timekeeper if time is a major constraint.
- Give a short summary or recap before going on to the next

area. Be sure people understand what the group has agreed to.

- End with an action step. Meetings fail because people aren't held accountable. Summarize the action steps the group members are to take and attach a time frame to each action. The only way to get commitment is to assign a deadline.

Giving a Motivational Keynote

What's the difference between a persuasive speech, a seminar, and a motivational keynote? Emotion and entertainment. The purpose of a motivational speech is to move emotions, inspire, and entertain. Think show biz. People will expect humor, so plan some funny anecdotes. But don't tell jokes unless you have experience doing stand-up comedy.

Keynotes are generally given to larger audiences. The challenge for you is to create intimacy in a large group. How do you do that?

- Begin with a warmup—an icebreaker or a beginning attempt at humor. Usually some self-deprecating humor helps the audience get to know you. One professional speaker who is 6 feet, 5 inches tall and has red hair and freckles references *The Andy Griffith Show* to create rapport with the audience. He introduces himself as "Opie on steroids."
- Tell the audience your objectives. Let listeners know where you're going and that there's a point to your motivational talk.
- Develop each point with a story. This is how the motivational speech differs from the persuasive talk. You tap into listeners' emotions. Essentially, you become a storyteller.
- Be prepared. Create short and long versions of each story. If your time is cut short, you can tell the one-minute story instead of the five-minute rendition.
- Be respectful of people's emotions. When you tell a tear-evoking story, immediately follow up with some humor. Don't

open the audience up unless you're willing to close them back up. One speaker I heard told such a heart-wrenching story that everyone was in tears at the end of his speech. The problem was we stayed tearful. The ending was a downer.

- Tell your own stories. It's unethical to tell someone else's stories without permission. The most effective stories are based on your own experiences.
- Don't embarrass people by using their names in a story without their permission.
- Develop a flair for drama. Practice vocal variety by softening your voice and then increasing the energy. Practice the pause. Listeners need to feel the impact of your words. They need time for things to sink in.
- End with your most powerful story. Leave the audience on a high by giving them a message of hope.

Conducting Seminars and Workshops

A seminar or workshop is skills-based. Audiences expect content that relates to their immediate needs. Whether your seminar is a half-day or a week in length, people will expect information they can use. They want practical skills and they'll look to you as the expert.

Seminars focus on new information, whereas workshops are training classes. When you're conducting a seminar or workshop, consider the following tips:

- Set clear learning objectives and get agreement from the group.
- Relate objectives and exercises to participants' needs. Audience members don't want fluff and they don't want a lot of theory.
- Take care of housekeeping items early. Mention break times, lunch, and the locations of rest rooms and phones.

- Build rapport. Begin with a story or humor to relax the audience. (Some people have "school anxiety" and have not been in a classroom since high school or college.)
- Establish your credibility early. You can do so through your introduction or by including a bio with your handouts.
- Develop materials. Most participants will expect handouts and/or workbooks.
- Create modules. These are similar to book chapters. For a financial planning seminar, modules might include "Financial Assessment," "Investment Instruments," and "Estate Planning." You can then divide these areas into subcategories.
- Time each module. "Financial Assessment" could be twenty minutes.
- Include in each module the learning objective, the concepts (lecture content), application (exercises for the learners), and a summary.
- Bridge from one module to another with a transition: "Now that you have a measure of your financial health, let's start to examine investment instruments."
- Use humor, but remember that the audience is there to learn.
- Use a variety of visual aids, such as overheads, slides, and flip charts. Post flip charts around the room to reinforce the learning points.
- Involve the audience. Too many instructors fall back on lecturing. Use a variety of training techniques, such as paired exercises, role plays, simulations, written exercises, quizzes, videotapes, games, and question and answer periods. People learn better when the process is "hands on."
- Provide a summary of each segment before you move on to the next area.
- End with a summary or upbeat motivational message. Ask attendees to complete their evaluations before they leave.

Doing One-to-One Presentations

Speaking to an individual is different from the group experience. Whether you're training someone, selling, coaching, or asking for a raise, here are some tips for speaking one-to-one:

- Eliminate distractions. Choose a comfortable setting—perhaps your office or a conference room with good lighting. Block off distracting window views and minimize interruptions. Clear the table of clutter.

- Sit next to the person at eye level. Sit side by side rather than across a desk from each other. This has psychological and physical effects. It creates a feeling of being on the same side and allows both people to look at materials from the same perspective.

- Maintain good eye contact but don't stare. In a group, you make eye contact with everyone. With individuals, you don't want to lock eyes. Break eye contact from time to time. A good guide is to look at the person 70% of the time.

- Use visual aids. Props, pictures, and objects can serve as effective visual aids. Visuals are important learning tools, and you shouldn't overlook them in a one-to-one situation. Be sure your visuals are appropriate to the situation. A few carefully placed props and occasional use of a table easel can enhance your presentation.

- Clarify but don't repeat questions. In a large group, you repeat the question so that everyone can hear it. But in one-to-one settings, the same technique would be silly. You may ask for clarification: "Are you saying that you need more practice?" Or you may restate the question in your answer: "The procedure for this project is..."

- Maintain a comfortable physical distance. Don't invade the other person's space. When sitting side by side, don't lean in or take over the person's materials. Ask permission to demonstrate with or alter their materials.

- Pause. The brain needs a few seconds to process information. Don't overload the learner with too much data. Pause between thoughts to let the information sink in.
- Use smaller gestures. Show enthusiasm and get involved with the learner. Allow yourself to be natural and expressive. But contain your gestures, because the physical space is smaller in one-to-one situations. Wide, sweeping movements will seem out of place.
- Prepare and organize. It's easy to lose track of time when you're working with only one person. Whether you train one person or a hundred, the preparation is the same. Without adequate preparation, you'll seem disorganized and unprofessional. Prepare an outline and establish time frames.
- Watch for nonverbal cues. In a group, different personalities react in diverse ways. Someone in the group will often say what others are thinking. In a one-to-one situation, however, the person may feel reluctant to tell you that he or she needs a break or doesn't understand. Watch for body language and continually check back: "You look like you disagree." "Are you ready for a break?" "Is this something you can use on the job?"

Delivering Sales Presentations

You can deliver sales presentations to groups, as part of a team, or individually. Since most selling situations are one-to-one, review the tips above for one-to-one presentations. Here are some additional tips for giving an effective sales presentation:

- Plan. Don't wing it just because you know your product and you've sold it to other customers. To make the sale, you need to know about the customer, his or her business, and his or her industry. Spend time researching your prospects.
- Establish an outcome. Sales presentations won't go anywhere

unless you have a clear objective. Do you want to close the sale? Set up a meeting to make a second presentation? Be sure your objectives are appropriate to the situation.

- Create rapport. This is important in any presentation, but it's absolutely critical in a sales presentation. People are guarded when dealing with a salesperson. Spend time getting to know their interests, and show genuine concern. Think relationship—not sale.
- Set an agenda. People are busy and don't want you to waste their time. Establish rapport and present an agenda: "I'd like to discuss your financial needs, review your portfolio, and then make some recommendations. It should take just under an hour." Providing an agenda gives the customer a road map and keeps you on target.
- Ask questions and search for needs. The more explicit the needs you uncover, the more successful you'll be. Prepare your questions in advance. Focus on the consequences of not taking action and the benefits of moving toward a solution. The quality of your questions determines the outcome of your sales presentation.
- Make it visual. Most people are visual. Seeing is believing. Refer to a diagram, show listeners a brochure, or sketch a diagram—but let people see what you have. A table easel is a good way to display your presentation. You can buy one at a good art supply store.
- Sell benefits, not features. Customers don't care about all the little details of how your product or service works. They want to know what it will do for them.
- Be conversational. Presentations are more effective when you're conversational. Nobody likes listening to a talking head. If people think you're scripted, you'll lose credibility.
- Listen, listen, listen. Selling is not pitching or talking. A sales presentation involves a lot of listening. You can *talk* your way out of a sale, but I've never heard of anyone *listening* his or her

way out of a sale. Clarify and rephrase your understanding of what your listeners have said. Acknowledge and empathize with the feelings of your prospective customers. Be quiet and listen.

- End with an action step. Summarize what you've discussed and then ask for commitment. An action step has a *what* and a *when*: "Let's set up an appointment with the management committee. How is Thursday at 2:00?" Be clear about what you want.

Making Impromptu Presentations

Mark Twain said it took about three weeks to make a good impromptu speech. Thinking on your feet may scare you. But you can improve with practice. At every job interview you've had, you've given an impromptu presentation. You prepared, of course, but you couldn't always anticipate every question.

Keep these ideas in mind for the next time you must make an impromptu presentation:

- Listen to the entire question. An impromptu talk usually happens when you must respond to a question: "How would you go about...?" or "Give us your thoughts on..." Let the person finish the question so that you understand it. If you don't understand the question, don't begin answering. Ask for clarification.
- Breathe and collect your thoughts. Don't rush to answer. Remember the pause! This gives you time to collect your thoughts. Pausing also looks professional—it shows that you're thinking your answer through.
- Be brief and concrete. An impromptu speech has a structure— a beginning, a middle, and an end. You must quickly organize your thoughts, state your idea or position, develop your idea with an example, and then end your response. Too much detail will overwhelm the listener. Practice answering within

one to two minutes.

- Practice. Toastmasters International has a segment at every meeting called Table Topics. Speakers have to speak "off the cuff" on a variety of topics. You can practice on your own. Have your friends write ten questions from current events. Let them ask you the questions so that you can practice answering. You'll gain confidence as you practice.

- Speak with confidence. Your voice conveys your emotional state. Do you snap out your answer? Are you mumbling or inaudible? Do you hesitate? Believe in what you say.

- Watch your body language. Listeners can tell more from your body language than from your words. Impromptu speaking is less formal and it's easy to forget your delivery skills. Stand or sit up straight, be enthusiastic, and smile. Maintain eye contact or you'll lose conviction.

- Create a clear ending. Many impromptu speakers do a good job answering the question, only to let it drop like a lead balloon at the end. An impromptu presentation needs an ending. You can end by repeating a point: "And that's why I take this view."

Participating in Media Interviews

You may be called upon to be an organizational spokesperson. Or you may promote your own business. Whatever the reason, when you're interviewed on radio or television, here are some key points to consider:

- Know the audience. Who listens to this station? Is it a business crowd, the general public, or a college audience? What's the focus of the show? Does it cover financial news, health issues, or women's topics?

- Know the difference between the show's host and its producer. Write down their names. It's embarrassing to call the host by the producer's name.

- Find an angle. Radio and TV interviewers are looking for good entertainment and good stories. They won't interview you unless your topic is newsworthy and of interest to the listeners. Write a headline for yourself. What's unusual or different about what you have to say? "Dog Bites Man" is a mundane story. "Man Bites Dog" is newsworthy. Tie your topic to an industry trend or current event. Make it interesting.
- Speak in sound bites. Being brief is more important in the media than in any other situation. If you have 15 to 30 seconds before you go to commercial, you'll need to speak concisely. Say it simply. Prepare your own questions and write out the answers using simple language. Eliminate polysyllabic words. Aim for a sixth-grade audience and prepare two- to three-minute segments of material. Television and radio are fast-paced. You won't have time to tell long stories.
- Don't respond with a simple yes or no. If asked, "Do you still get nervous speaking?" say, "Yes. In fact, last night I rehearsed and gave myself a pep talk. The only difference is now I'm trained to channel my nervousness."
- Check the backdrop color for TV appearances. I once wore a raspberry suit only to find out that the backdrop was orange. The colors bled together and looked awful on videotape. Certain colors do not televise well. Don't wear black, white (too much reflected light), red, kelly green, patterns, or certain icy pastels. Most shades of blue photograph well.
- Look at the interviewer. Let the camera do its job. Speak to the interviewer, not the camera. The camera people will get the shots they want. Remember: you're having a conversation with the host.

For some radio shows, you'll be interviewed by phone. If so:

- Don't use a cell phone. You can experience electronic interference that will make it difficult for listeners to hear you.

- Don't play the radio in the background during your interview or have someone listen in on an extension. This can interfere with the quality of the broadcast.
- Keep the studio phone number handy. If the producer doesn't call you on time, you may have to call him or her. Something may have happened. Or the person may have lost your number.
- Don't read! When you're being interviewed by phone, it's tempting to read from a paper. Don't. The audience can sense when you're scripted. Be conversational.
- Assume the microphone is always on. Watch what you say during breaks. You could be picked up without knowing it, and that could be embarrassing.

Videoconferencing

Videoconferencing is a presentation. You may be conducting a meeting with your regional office. Or maybe you're going to Kinko's to schedule a videoconference with your friend overseas. The setup may include one or two cameras and several speaker phones. You'll be seated at a conference table and you'll have to coordinate speaking from both sites.

Consider these guidelines when you're presenting through videoconferencing:

- Prepare and organize. Prepare a checklist for participating speakers. Go over visuals, schedules, procedures, equipment, and agendas.
- Rehearse with the participants so that they know what to expect.
- Appoint a moderator if appropriate. The moderator will introduce guests and keep the presentation flowing.
- Appoint a person to operate the controls. This frees you to communicate instead of changing slides or going in for a close-up.

- Minimize distractions. Keep noise down by restricting movement in and out of the room. Hold all telephone calls. Turn off personal beepers.
- Respect timing. Don't go over your time limit or you'll impact the other presentations. Focus on key points and stick to the agenda.
- Dress for television. Avoid dangling jewelry, shiny clothing, and wide patterns. Find out the background color of the conference room and dress accordingly.
- Speak into the camera. The camera is your audience when you're speaking. When a discussion takes place, you can look at the moderator. When you're addressing an individual, speak directly to that person.
- Explain what's going on. The people on the other end can't see everything in the room. Ask them if they understand what's been said and answer questions as they come up.
- Pause. Expect time delays. If the video signal is weak, there could be a delay in the video transmission. That means your voice and image may not always be in sync. This may take some getting used to. Keep in mind that your actions will be amplified when you move or wave your hands, so don't make any sudden, abrupt, or sweeping movements.
- Rent space if your organization doesn't provide videoconferencing. You can schedule time at Kinko's or another off-site facility. Kinko's has sites internationally. You schedule the time and length of the conference and then show up the day of the presentation. The other person broadcasts from his or her local Kinko's.
- Try desktop videoconferencing for convenience. This will become more popular in the next few years. It requires that you purchase a tiny video attachment for your laptop. The receiver must also have the same equipment. You'll see a head shot in the corner of your laptop computer. You may need to wear a special earpiece or headset. Don't expect studio quality.

Taking the Next Step

Congratulations! You've completed the journey to effective public speaking. You now have a road map to guide you through your next presentation. And I want to know how it goes. You have the skills. Now go out and do it.

Let me know about your success stories as well as your challenges. You can contact me at:

DiResta Communications
P.O. Box 140714
Staten Island, NY 10314
(718) 273-8627
Web: http://www.diresta.com
E-mail: diane@diresta.com

To make this a truly interactive experience, I invite you to take advantage of a free ten-minute coaching call to get your presentation off to a strong start.

I know you'll be a knockout!

Appendix of Resources

Professional Associations

American Society for Training and Development (ASTD)
1640 King Street
P.O. Box 1443
Alexandria, VA 22313-2043
(703) 683-8100
Fax: (703) 683-8103
http://www.astd.org
This association for training professionals provides local monthly
meetings, a magazine, special interest groups, and a library of the
latest training and development technology. It is an excellent
resource for any speaker who wants current information on the
education and seminar industry.

American Speech-Language-Hearing Association (ASHA)
10801 Rockville Pike
Rockville Pike, MD 20852-3279

(800) 498-2071

Fax: (301) 571-0457

Web: http://www.asha.org

ASHA is the professional association for speech pathologists, audiologists, and language specialists. Although it is clinical in nature, ASHA provides a nationwide referral service. Speakers who want to improve their voice and diction can easily find a trained professional in their area.

National Speakers Association (NSA)

1500 S. Priest Drive

Tempe, AZ 85281

(602) 968-2552

Fax: (602) 968-0911

Web: http://www.nsaspeaker.org

NSA is the premier association for professional speakers. For any one who is a paid speaker or wants to break into the business, membership is a must. They provide a magazine, audiotape, special interest groups, electronic bulletin boards and chat rooms, an annual convention, and a winter workshop. The focus is on building a speaking business. There are also local chapters in your area.

Toastmasters International

P.O. Box 9052

Mission Viejo, California 92690

(949) 858-8255

Fax: (949) 858-1207

Web: http://www.toastmasters.org

Toastmasters is an organization dedicated to improving public speaking. There are monthly meetings, conferences, and contests. For a nominal membership fee, they provide a workbook to practice speeches. At every meeting, members experience the roles of toastmaster (MC), speaker, evaluator, and more. It is a wonderful organization for anyone at any level who wants to enhance their speaking skills.

International Listening Association
P.O. Box 25324
Overland Park, KS 66225-5324
(800) ILA-4505
ILA is an association dedicated to the study and promotion of listening at all levels. Their annual conference provides workshops and information on current research, listening training in the school, in business, and in personal relationships. ILA produces a quarterly research journal for members.

Training Materials

Creative Training Techniques International
7620 West 78th Street
Edina, MN 55439-2518
(800) 383-9210
Fax: (612) 829-0260
Web: http://www.cctbobpike.com
This training company produces a catalog of training products such as videos, games, books, markers, and audio cassettes to add spark to your presentations. For copyright free music you can play before, during, or after your presentation, ask for Powerful Presentation Music.

Paper Direct
100 Plaza Drive
Secaucus, NJ 07094-3606
(800) 272-7377
Web: http://www.paperdirect.com
Paper Direct is a company that supplies ready-made paper templates for brochures, certificates, flyers, table top easels and other related items to help you promote your presentation.

Phobia Treatment

The Institute of NLP, Inc.
8820 Business Park Drive, Suite 400
Austin, TX 78759-7456
(800) 499-2156
Web: http://www.fmp.com/mastery
Neurolinguistic programming is a technology that can be very useful for treating traumas or phobias as well as developing communication skills. In rare cases, you may require the help of a counselor to alleviate the fear of speaking. The NLP Institute can provide you with a list of practitioners in your area.

Evaluate Your Presentation

The goal of this book is to make you your own coach. Use this form to evaluate your next presentation. Videotape yourself or rate yourself from memory immediately after the speech using a 1-to-10 scale, with 10 as highest and 1 as lowest. As you grade yourself, think about the recommendations given in this book. Use them as benchmarks for grading your performance. Give yourself credit for your strengths. Identify the areas needing improvement and reread the exercises for those skills.

	Rating	Notes
Delivery	**1-10**	
Posture	_____	_____
Purposeful Movement	_____	_____
Image/Appearance	_____	_____
Confident Language	_____	_____
Eye Contact	_____	_____
Gestures	_____	_____

Intonation   _____   _____

Enthusiasm   _____   _____

Facial Expression   _____   _____

Pausing   _____   _____

Speaking Rate   _____   _____

Non-words (ah, um)   _____   _____

Uptalk (pitch rises)   _____   _____

Q&A Control   _____   _____

Organization

Strong Opening   _____   _____

Clear Benefits   _____   _____

Strong Evidence   _____   _____

Logical Sequence   _____   _____

Main Points Developed   _____   _____

Transitions   _____   _____

Visual Aids   _____   _____

Strong Closing   _____   _____

Informative   _____   _____

Persuasive   _____   _____

Recommended Reading

Ailes, Roger, *You Are the Message: Getting What You Want by Being Who You Are* (New York: Doubleday, 1988).

Axtell, Roger E., *Do's and Taboos Around the World*, 3rd Edition (New York: John Wiley & Sons, Inc. 1993).

Brandt, Richard C., *Flip Charts: How to Draw Them and How to Use Them* (Pfieffer & Co., 1987).

Burley-Allen, Madelyn, *Listening: The Forgotten Skill,* 2nd Edition (New York: John Wiley & Sons, 1995).

Currid, Cheryl, *Make Your Point! The Complete Guide to Successful Business Presentations Using Today's Technology* (Rocklin, CA: Prima Publishing, 1995).

Klinkenberg, Hilka, *At Ease Professionally: An Etiquette Guide for the Business Arena* (Chicago: Bonus Books, 1992).

Laborde, Genie Z., *Influencing with Integrity* (Palo Alto, CA: Syntony, 1983).

Leeds, Dorothy, *Powerspeak: The Complete Guide to Persuasive Public Speaking and Presenting* (New York: Berkley, 1991).

Maloney, Stephen R., *Talk Your Way to the Top: Communication Secrets of the CEOs* (Englewood Cliffs, NJ: Prentice Hall, 1992).

Mindell, Phyllis, *A Woman's Guide to the Language of Success* (Englewood Cliffs, N.J: Prentice Hall, 1995).

Montgomery, Robert L., *Listening Made Easy: How to Improve Listening on the Job, at Home, and in the Community* (New York, AMACOM, 1987).

Sarnoff, Dorothy, *Never Be Nervous Again* (New York: Ivy Books, 1987).

Schloff, Laurie and Marcia Yudkin, *Smart Speaking: 60-Second Strategies for More than 100 Speaking Problems and Fears* (New York, Penguin, 1991).

Steil, Lyman K., Larry L. Barker, and Kittie W. Watson, *Effective Listening: Key to Your Success* (Reading, MA: Addison-Wesley, 1983).

Walters, Lilly, *Secrets of Successful Speakers: How You Can Motivate, Captivate, and Persuade* (New York: McGraw Hill, 1993).

Index